CW00972122

friendshipfirst
the manual

*Ordinary Christians
discussing
good news with
ordinary Muslims*

Steve Bell

Friendship First Publications

First published in 2003

ISBN 0-9544063-0-3

Produced by
Friendship First
P.O. Box 170, Market Rasen LN8 3WB UK
Email: friendship2101@aol.com

Acknowledgements

Thanks firstly go to Action Partners Ministries for allowing me the opportunity to start work on this manuscript during a sabbatical.

I have always found Colin Chapman's company stimulating and his approach to Islam helpful. I have adapted some of his pegs to hang some of my own ideas on in this volume. These are particularly borrowed from '*You go and do the Same*' and a little from '*The Cross & the Crescent*'.

I am also grateful to Andrew Smith (alias "Smeee"), for his helpful comments, and for kindly sharing with me the 'flavour' of his findings from the world of young British Muslims. His insights stopped me being even more unbalanced, especially when it comes to the delicate issue of how to "accommodate" a Muslim's views and culture without "compromise" of the gospel.

Thanks also to Bill Musk, who, ever since we have known one another, has consistently modelled for me, the 'grace response' to Muslim people. He has been kind enough to take the time to read the manuscript and make comment on, what for him is a 'low brow' (if innovative) piece compared to his normal domain within the discipline.

I am grateful to David Sladden for being the iron to sharpen iron. His incisive comments proved invaluable - even when he took a different view to me. I was often forced to think again, to clarify, to qualify and even on occasions to justify my thinking. The manual is the better for it.

Thanks to Don Rowley of WEC for being Paul to this Timothy. Also to Martin & Elizabeth Goldsmith for their friendship and for Martin's ability to teach me how to think missiologically. Then to Jack & Monica (Abu wa Oum Philip) Blockley for their comments, encouragement, unfailing example of Christian living; but above all for unknowingly demonstrating that - given several decades - it is possible for Westerners to assimilate almost seamlessly into Arabic society.

To my wife Julia for unending support and for alerting me when my head has been in the manuscript or the Koran for too long at a stretch. Also to the various readers and checkers. A huge "thank you".

Finally to Him for whom all this has been prepared. May He take its content and so change the attitudes of 'ordinary' Christians that they will be compelled to develop friendly relationships with 'ordinary' Muslims.

Steve Bell
'Fairways' - March 2003

Contents

Material about Islam tends to concentrate on the technical issues involved in Islam as a religion. There is a need for something less technical and more focussed on Muslims as people. This manual is an attempt to do just that by reversing this emphasis in order to introduce to the market, something, which helps 'ordinary' Christians to discuss good news with 'ordinary' Muslims in an atmosphere of friendship.

Friendship First is intended to be a conciliatory approach to Muslims as people. Although not intended for Muslims to read, it should not unduly offend a Muslim. It could even be useful to a Muslim who is actively enquiring about the Gospel. However, it is written specifically for 'ordinary' Christians with the realisation that it is the 'ordinary' Christians who rub shoulders with 'ordinary' Muslims in the work-a-day world, not the mission specialists or academics.

The magazine format, is not designed to be read straight through, but rather makes it easier to browse and retrieve information as the need arises from conversations with a Muslim friend.

The traditional image of a Muslim has been the old devout man with a long white beard and prayer beads studying the Koran in an ornate mosque. This is only one piece of the mosaic of Muslims in The West. In reality, a significant proportion of Western Muslims are young people or young professionals who want to be integrated into society. They live in a twilight zone between Islamic and local culture. This manual attempts to help you grasp this reality of Westernised Muslims of the 21st Century. I pray that your response to the Muslim God leads you to, will be the motto - "Friendship First".

Setting the Scene

"True tolerance is to accept the other, not by ignoring the distance between us, but by measuring that distance accurately and by recognizing that whoever wants to cross over has the right and the freedom to do so. Only love can create the necessary conditions for the truth to emerge…"

Chawkat Moucarry

International intelligence sources are now saying that 11 September 2001 was not an attack to end all terrorism but Al-Qaeda's declaration of the beginning of a final 'war on the West' for it's godlessness and interference in Muslim lands. Even some respected Bible scholars are saying that 9/11 triggered the beginning of countdown to the end and will likely culminate in the second coming of Christ.

With this sort of talk in mind it is both the worst time, and the best time, to talk about 'ordinary Christians' discussing the Gospel with 'ordinary Muslims'.

The Worst of times

This is the worst of times because people are understandably afraid of politicised Islam, which looks set to get worse. Akin to Joshua's campaigns to settle ancient Israel, at its best, the Islamic system is motivated by a vision, which is similar to the church. Islam lives for the worldwide rule of God called *khalifa*. This is a sort of Islamic "kingdom of God" on earth.

At its worst, politicised Islam gives the understandable impression that it has at its core, a mixture of demonic darkness and human determination to achieve worldwide political dominance; and that Islam waits menacingly to brutalise non-Muslims and turn the West into an Islamic society. It is not easy to deny this impression nor to hide the fact that the open political agenda of a minority of Muslims is to "re-educate" post-christian culture. Neither can we play down the evidence from Islamic heartlands of intolerance, harshness and repression, which have earned Islam the reputation of being the easiest religion to get into but the hardest to get out of.

Even some Christian leaders are suggesting that the West's spiritual vacuum will be eventually filled by Islam as it becomes Islamic. While it is true that Islam, like the

Setting the Scene

gay lobby, has an influence out of all proportion to its size, this claim seems to be a logical impossibility for the following reasons…

Social & political reasons

- To think that Islam will fill the spiritual vacuum in the West is to abandon the possibility of a Christian 'spiritual awakening'.

- In the sovereignty of God Islam was turned back by force of arms at Paris and Vienna in the Middle Ages. It would only be by divine providence that Islam should conquer Europe now.

- Many moderate Muslim lands have not achieved Islamic Law, how much less the West with its longstanding deeply embedded Judeo-Christian ethos?

- A haemorrhage is going on as the younger generation of Muslims are choosing to become westernised in values and lifestyle. This looks set to increase.

- Islam is only the fastest growing religion on earth because of its high birth rate. This must be compared with the church being the front-runner in conversion growth.

Ideological reasons

- Islam's culture-bound assumptions about the world are diametrically opposed to Western cultural instincts.

- Islam is a totally deistic (God-centred) worldview. It may be easier for America to have a Communist revolution than for the post-modern West to embrace Islam. The latest national census is expected to show 5,000 white Britons who have embraced Islam and 50,000 practising Buddhism, so which is the "threat"?

- Muslim leaders are going on record about the economic failure throughout the Muslim World. They are faced with the question 'Does Islam work in the modern world?'. The West remains the Muslim World's provider of technology and information.

- Islam's anti-feminist, anti-gay and male-dominant stance on gender roles is a clash.

- Islam's inability to scrutinize its own sources nor entertain any other comparative thought systems examining it is a clash.

- Islam's incompatibility with international human rights and the non-negotiable freedom of speech and of the individual is a clash.

Having said all this, it is still sometimes hard not to privately resent Western governments' apparent support for Muslim development and to suffer an irrational fear of Islamic take-over. Nevertheless, the challenge, which Christians face in light of these issues, is to keep the words "Islam" and "Muslim" in separate mental compartments and to resist the suspicion of 'ordinary Muslims'. Many older Muslims are here for a quiet life away from the difficulties of their homelands while the younger generation often want to be accepted as Western.

Photo courtesy of AWM International ©

Statistics

While most Muslims are peace-loving people, the following is true of political Islam…

- *90% of all refugees are from the Muslim World*

- *Of the 30 conflicts going on in the world, 28 are in Muslim lands*

- *Of the 25 countries where human rights violations are going on against non-conformists, 21 are Muslim states*

Setting the Scene

Christians are seen by Muslims as being "People of the Book". This means they are not Muslims of the house of submission (Dar al-Islam) nor are they "unbelievers" (Dar al-Harb). Christians are in an almost unique position to walk out onto the bridge of friendship, which spans the chasm between Islam and Western society. Like few others, it is a Christian who can meet the Muslim half way in the name of the Lord who said

'The…God of gods… shows love to the foreigners living among you…You too, must show love to foreigners' (Deut 10:17).

This manual attempts to explain how we can put this command into practise by personally moving from "resentment" to "tolerance" and then to "love".

'We feel deeply the humiliation, the marginalisation of the whole Muslim world. Muslim countries are so divided, so small, so irrelevant… We are the most backward among nations, and the poorest. Almost the whole of Islam belongs to the Third World. Part of the Middle East may have enormous oil resources, but, even there it is the West that ultimately controls them'.

Dr Zaki Badawi, Chairman of the British Council of Mosques

The Best of times

This is also the best of times for 'ordinary Christians' to humbly discuss the Good News with 'ordinary Muslims'. Worldwide, issues are being brought to bear, which are pressuring the household of Islam towards reform (*islah*). The global insistence on human rights suggests that, in the end Islam will not undergo reform *a la* Al-Qaeda (i.e. forced retreat into mediaeval violence) but rather reform *a la* the growing majority of moderate Muslims (i.e. to move temperately forward as a religion in the 21st Century).

Whatever the future, this manual offers a 'grace response' to Muslims who had no choice about being born into a system, which may be more humanly conceived than divinely inspired. A 'grace response' means being prepared to see beyond the apparent human construction and the problematic sources, to the God of all grace, to whom millions of sincere Muslims are reaching out for solace and reassurance in this life and the hereafter.

No matter how negative the media images of Islam become, God's "outrageous grace" is extended towards Muslim people, as it is to all peoples everywhere. In fact there is evidence that God may be drawing Muslims to Christ now more than at any time in Islam's history. In this respect, things are set to get even better. So let's not panic. The same sovereign Lord who oversaw Islam's arrival on the world

Setting the Scene

1

> *…'even to this day whenever the old covenant is being read, a veil covers their minds so they cannot understand the truth. And this veil can only be removed by believing in Christ…But whenever anyone turns to the Lord, then the veil is taken away.'*
>
> *2 Cors 3:14,16*

stage continues to guide history to His appointed end. Islam cannot be beyond God's sovereignty.

A grace response to Muslims is also crucial because, as we shall see, it can be argued that Islam is in some ways an Arabised form of Judaism. This is due to its roots in Abraham and the Old Testament Semitic culture of the Middle East. It adopts the Torah and forms its own Sharia Law, it venerates the Jewish prophets, its males are circumcised, it has a lunar calendar. The call of the minaret replaces the call of the rams horn (shofar).

These features bring Muslims closer to Christians than is comfortable for either. This is why Islam (unwittingly) has the effect of partly evangelising a Muslim by instilling into him or her some of the basic building blocks of the gospel. If this is the case, many Muslims probably live in a 'pre-evangelised' state. If the Holy Spirit were to 'lift the floodgates' and move in power, potentially millions of Muslims could one day find themselves swept over the line into the Kingdom of God. Should such an ingathering happen, Muslims could be the Gentiles who fulfil the Apostle Paul's predictions of *'provoking the Jews to jealousy' (Roms 10:19, 11:11).*

We are now likely to be in the closing days of history. Muslim people (i.e. followers of the religion of the Arab sons of Ishmael), like Jewish sons of Isaac, are starting to come to Christ worldwide. Proof of this came home to me when a British believer in Jesus from a Muslim background told me that she discovers more Muslim conversions to Christ on her trips back to Asia than she knows of in the West - where it is supposed to be easier to convert. Western Christians must be ready to respond to friendships and to be able, confidently and humbly, to give account of their faith to enquiring Muslims.

Photo courtesy of AWM International ©

> *'Christ, in his dealings with ordinary people around him, tended to free them from the 'ideal' religion of the professionals. Why educate the ordinary Muslims in their own faith so that Christ can meet them there tomorrow when he can meet them more fundamentally at the point of their felt-needs today?'*
>
> *Bill Musk*

Setting the Scene

New Approach to Muslims

Many books about Islam tend to be fairly academic. This can happen because the focus is on Islam as a religion rather than how to discuss the Good News with Muslims as people. In the past, keen Christians have often found themselves inadvertently teaching Muslims more about Islam than about the grace of God in Christ. As a grace response to Muslim people, this manual tries to explain clearly how to relate to the Muslim as an individual without the overtones of cultural or spiritual superiority.

> *Our aim is that we relate to Muslims in such a way that the only offence we cause is that of the Cross.*

To do this we will take a relational approach. The apostle Paul's conscious commitment to relationships with people is described in his first letter to the Corinthian church.

We will be taking, what is called, an 'apologetic' approach. This means a commitment to teasing out points, which help us connect with a Muslim rather than push us further apart. This helps construct the bridge on which to meet the Muslim in order to discuss the Good News about Jesus. The opposite approach is called the 'polemic' approach. This tends to emphasise differences and contradictions, which promotes arguments. The danger is that it can end up with rhetoric being shouted across the chasm of differences between us. In this case a Muslim would be better off never meeting a Christian. This will not do. The balance to be sought is that we do everything that the Gospel requires of us without compromising with Islam.

> *Often our first step is to recognise we have an attitude problem!*

This manual is intended to be a user-friendly resource. Going out onto that bridge is a risky business but these are risks we must be prepared to take. The manual breaks new ground in order to motivate ordinary Christians to develop genuine relationships with ordinary Muslims.

Photo courtesy of Frontiers International ©

> '...I have become a servant of everyone so that I can bring them to Christ. When I am with the Jews, I become one of them... When I am with those who follow Jewish laws, I do the same, even though I am not subject to the law...When I am with the Gentiles who do not have the Jewish law, I fit in with them as much as I can. In this way I gain their confidence...Yes I try to find common ground with everyone so that I might bring them to Christ'.
>
> *1 Cors 9:19-33*

Setting the Scene

I hope that the manual will not so much 'inform' as 'affect' the reader. It is not so much an A,B,C of Islam as an A, E, I, O, U of friendship with a Muslim. This is to say it is aimed at affecting your…

A - attitude

We are still, in part, a class-conscious society. This includes various forms of polite and even overt racism. The British Commission for Racial Equality has done its work during a period when "institutional racism" has been found everywhere from the police to the armed forces. Although words like "Greasy Dago", "Paki", "Wog", "Coon" or "Taliban" may be heard less, there is a swing going on towards the political right. This seems to be a reaction to understandable fears about continued immigration and the potential of 'swamping' the national identity and resources. It is becoming a social statement for a Christian to have a welcoming attitude to an immigrant, let alone an asylum-seeker or refugee.

E - emotions

Some Christians, actually resent the presence of Muslims in the West. An important step towards genuine relationship with a Muslim is to recognise that many of us hold such subconscious feelings towards them - and some of them towards us. We must deal with negative emotions - particularly fear and resentment. Emotions are often stirred up because of our underlying attitudes; for example that Muslim culture is somehow inferior to our way of life. It comes as a surprise to some people that some aspects of Muslim culture are more biblical, and therefore "civilised" than the Western morality of convenience. This manual will help you to discover how to become more open to God's heart and mind with regard to the 'ordinary Muslim'.

I - information

When we have faced our attitude and emotions we are in a better position to receive accurate information about Muslims. For example, as we have said earlier, the fact that they are adherents of a religious tradition that could be described as an Arabised form of Judaism. This claim is based on the fact that Islam identifies itself with the Old Testament Torah and that the Five Pillars of Islam are Old Testament practices rooted in Abraham. A Muslim, like a Jew, therefore carries potential sensitivity to the Gospel due to their acceptance of the following foundational ideas contained in the Gospel - God, Christ, submission, the will of God, prayer, fasting, godly living, heaven, hell and judgement. As such, Muslims, like Jews, are in need of the completion of some of their religious practise in Christ.

Setting the Scene

Muslims follow an Arabised form of Judaism and as such are in need of the completion of their faith in Christ.

O - opportunities

Only then can we be in a position to take advantage of the increasing God-given opportunities with ordinary Muslims, especially since 11 September 2001. Muslims need God-fearing Westerners who they can trust. Ordinary Muslims need ordinary Christians to get alongside them. The Bible says that it is God who oversees human history and the migration of peoples around the planet (Acts 17:26-27). So one of the reasons Muslims are in the West is to find faith in Jesus Christ.

'The church has been unsuccessful in bringing Muslims to Christ for hundreds of years. We have tried to evangelise them, found it hard and labelled them difficult and resistant, rather than questioning our Western presumptions about how to communicate the gospel effectively to them in terms they can understand'.

Giulio Basetti-Sani

U - understanding

The result of all of the above is that our understanding of Muslims can develop to the extent that we can become effective witnesses to the grace of God in Jesus Christ.

Wrong Ideas about Islam

Photo courtesy of Frontiers International©

For too long we have been getting it wrong when it comes to relating the Good News of Jesus to Muslims. This is partly due to the fact that we are negatively affected by media stereotypes based on the minority of Muslim extremists. A senior denominational leader said to me "Islam is a specialist area isn't it?"

"I knew a Muslim family which, due to a tragedy, had left their homeland. One evening my wife and I visited them. After fun-filled interaction with the children, I asked how they were enjoying my home country. We found they had been in the country a year but had never seen the inside of a home. They were lonely and eager for friendship. The sad thing was there were Bible-believing churches close by. Not one church member had called on this family'.

This is partly a result of the material on Islam, which has tended to be fairly technical. As a result, sincere Christians have tended to assume that some 'expert' should do it.

Wrong attitudes to Muslims

A man once asked me "Would you give me some hints on how to give the gospel to a Muslim at work". He was visibly surprised to get the answer "No". He retorted "But you are the expert on it aren't you?" A deal was struck with him. "When you can come and ask how to discuss the gospel with your Muslim *friend*, I can help you". The biggest step in relating the Good News to a Muslim is when we step away from confrontation and towards genuine friendship.

Become a real friend to a Muslim!

Photo courtesy of AWM International©

Spiritual hunger leads them

There are no short cuts. It is now clear from research that the spiritually thirsty Muslim, like anyone else, is drawn to the person of Jesus Christ by a mixture of 'heart-hunger' and intellectual curiosity. Muslims should not be seen as Jehovah's Witnesses whose doctrine needs correcting. Remember Islam is culturally Semitic and therefore, partially at least, a more biblical worldview than the West's.

Islam seems to lead Muslims to the Islamic wellhead. However, like the Woman at the Well in John's Gospel, the well is deep and there is no bucket to draw with (John 4). The scent of 'living' water may be there but the human traditions, which have developed over the centuries within Islam, deny them a drink from Jesus Christ. Like the Apostle Paul in his letter to the Roman church, many Muslims sigh inwardly out of weariness from trying to live out religious regulations in their own strength …*"Oh what a miserable person I am! Who will free me from this life that is dominated by sin?"* (Rom 7:24).

A potential open door is the fact that Muslims are encouraged by the Koran to relate to Jews and Christians (i.e. People of the Book) in *'the best possible way'* (*Sura 29:46; 3:64**). Through friendship with a Muslim we can steer away from old point-scoring attitudes, on both sides. This is a relational approach whereby a Muslim friend can begin from where he or she is and start to unearth the signposts pointing to Jesus that were there all the time, even within Islam.

*n.b. All quotes from the Koran will look like this - (S3:16). This means "Sura" or chapter 3 and "Aya" or verse 16.

What is
a Muslim?

Photos courtesy of Frontiers International and AWM International ©

The ideal image of Muslims include wise old men with long beards sitting cross-legged on carpeted floors in ornate mosques studying the open Koran while they clutch their prayer beads. These images have become misleading because Islam in the West is now multi-faceted. Today a large proportion of Muslims are under 25 years of age, they are often very integrated into Western consumer fashion and values. This emerging generation includes young aspiring professionals and students who are at home in contemporary youth culture.

This stark contrast from the old to the young Muslim serves to mark the two ends of a spectrum of Western Muslims. It is almost impossible to hold the spread in tension. In between these two generations there are still more differences. There are 'non-religious' Muslims - these are often intellectual or secular. There are 'moderate' Muslims - these are often middle-of-the-road and more liberal. There are 'conservative' Muslims - these are often devout in belief and practise. There are 'radical' Muslims - these tend to be hard line and more extreme. Finally there are the 'Islamists' - these are the radical revolutionaries such as Al-Qaeda. It is virtually impossible to write anything that will equally apply to all these types. Having said that, here are some broad guidelines.

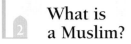

What is a Muslim?

Most Muslims fall into the following categories

NON-RELIGIOUS	non-practising, Islam is their conscience
OPEN	other religions are fine, all religion pleases God
MODERATE	Islam is best but others are tolerated
TRADITIONAL	nominal and uninformed
CONSERVATIVE	Islam is the best religion
RADICAL	Islam is the only valid religion
ISLAMIST	Islam must be implemented globally at all costs

What comes into your head when you think of a Muslim? Whatever it is will help identify your personal attitude towards them. Attitudes are dependent on previous experience of Muslims - or lack of it. Simply put, your attitude can only be positive, negative or indifferent. Which one do you think is your attitude? In reality though, most people find their attitude is a mixture of all three. How do the following images make you feel?

Negative stereotypes of Islam

- Al-Qaeda
- Palestinian activists
- The Taliban
- the Gulf War
- Saddam Hussein
- oil riches controlled by ruling families while the masses are poor
- mass prayer line-ups
- totalitarian regimes
- women in 'purdah'

Some of the images above involve individual Muslims. However, a Muslim is not Islam *per se* in the same way that someone living in Cuba is not Communism. Have you ever had a compassionate response to Muslims who have suffered from Islamic political regimes? Here are some positive stereotypes of Islam and Muslims as people.

Photo courtesy of Interserve ©

'If Islam is such a good system to live under, why are so many Muslims leaving Muslim lands?'

What is a Muslim?

2

Positive stereotypes of Muslims

- commitment to family values and responsibilities
- morally based and God-centred
- sincere religious practice
- modesty of dress and behaviour
- usually hard working
- beautiful architecture
- saintly old Muslim scholars
- tolerant Muslim spokespersons
- suffering victims in Bosnia and northern Iraq
- calligraphy

A letter from a Muslim thanking Mary Whitehouse CBE for her Christian stand for moral standards on TV
- *Christian Herald 18 May 2002*

'As a Muslim believer, I was, over the years, inspired and moved by her holy campaign to protect our children and all our society; to us Muslims, her campaign is an Islamic campaign and our duty, as Muslim believers, is to join her in her campaign and to support her all the time.

I believe our Muslim leaders and Imams have failed and neglected the huge damage, which can be caused by our immoral media and sexually sick and obsessed society.

I wanted so much to say to Mary before she died: Thank you for what you have done, thank you for alerting us Muslims to this great danger, thank you for giving us the hope that we can do a lot and make a change in our society'.

Dr A Majid Katme (Islamic Concern, Palmers Green, London)

2 | What is a Muslim?

Photo Steve Bell ©

Bible compels us to relate to strangers:

(Acknowledgement - Colin Chapman '*You go and do the same*')

Reading the following verses, how would you answer these questions?

Exodus 22:21; 23:9 *Leviticus19:33-34* *Deut 10:17-20*	What are the implications of these verses for us in the West today? What must it feel like to be an immigrant?
Matthew 5:43-48	"Love your neighbour" means those beyond your own community. How do you feel about that?
Matthew 7:12	How would you like your Muslim neighbour to treat you/your community? How does this affect the way you treat them?
Acts 9:10-19	What lay behind Ananias' doubts and suspicions? Are they similar to yours?
Acts 10:1-48	What was Peter's mental blockage? Do you have similar prejudice?
Galatians 1:21-24	Do you really believe that Muslims can change allegiance to Jesus?
1 Timothy 2:1-6	How closely does Paul's description of Jewish devotion resemble Muslims?

Thinking 'Christianly' about Muslims

Muslims are firstly people in the world for whom the Bible says Jesus Christ died. Our attitude must therefore be based on the Bible view of humankind.

1. We are not totally corrupt but all of our nature is affected by corruption in every area of life. Even the worship of God must be tainted according to Paul's observation about human nature - "*In me dwells no good thing*" (Romans 7:18).

2. A remnant of God remains in all humankind, including Muslims who are born just outside the Judeo-Christian revelation. Unlike many Westerners, Muslims are not godless. For this reason most Muslims are concerned about Jesus, but he is a figure who sadly bears little resemblance to the New Testament person. They are so near yet so far from the authentic Jesus.

If we scratch where Muslims are not itching we will only irritate them

What is a Muslim?

2

Diversity of Muslims

A Muslim is not a Muslim is not a Muslim. They come from very diverse racial groupings. They can often be quite 'foreign' to each other. We have to realise that Muslims have needs, which are quite specific to their grouping and background. These days many Muslims, whether born in the West or not, feel like 'strangers in the midst' in the biblical sense. They are not alone - so was Joseph in Egypt (Gen 37:12-36; 39-50), Ruth in Israel (Book of Ruth), the Exiles (see Psalm 137) and Paul in apostolic travelling (Acts 13-14, 16-20, 28:1-10). Here are some of the ways in which Muslims differ from each other.

Status

- refugees
- asylum seekers
- economic migrants
- foreign students
- resident immigrants
- Westernised 2nd generation

Race

- Indo-Pakistan sub-continent - India, Pakistan, Bangladesh
- Middle East - Egyptian, Palestinian, Kurdish, Irani, Iraqi, Jordanian
- Gulf - Yemeni, Emirates, Saudi
- North Africa - Moroccan, Algerian, Tunisian, Libyan
- Africa - Somali, Nigerian
- Europe - Bosnian, Turkish
- SE Asia - Malaysian, Philippino, Singaporian, Indonesian

We need to develop sensitivity to this diversity of race, nationality and culture.

'Do not exploit the foreigners who live in your land. They should be treated like everyone else, and you must love them as you love yourself...' (Lev 19:33-34).

'...I was a stranger and you invited me into your home' (Mat 25:35).

Language

Muslims speak many languages that can be quite foreign to one another.
- Asians may speak Urdu, Gujerati, Baluchi, Pashtu or Farsi
- Middle Easterners may speak a dialect of Arabic or Kurdish
- Europeans may speak Russian, Serbian, Albanian or Turkish
- Africans may speak Hausa, Bantu, Somali or Swahili

2 What is a Muslim?

Generations

In the West the under 30 year old Muslims tend to be more culturally assimilated, therefore they may hold to Islam less tightly - if at all; to the sadness of their parents.

This developing face of Islam in the West relates to comedians like Ali G. These Muslims are the MTV Rap generation. The socially marginalised young Muslim often finds in Islam, a racial and cultural identity. Islam becomes a coping mechanism in, what can be, a hostile society - especially post 9/11.

On the other hand, middle-aged and elderly Muslims tend to genuinely adhere to Islam more strongly as a means of cultural familiarity in, what they perceive to be, the 'godless' West.

Photo courtesy of Steve Bell©

Photo courtesy of AWM International©

'It's not been easy living round here. You feel you are being watched and judged all the time. If it's not your family, it's the people in the community. If it's not them it's the police.'

Najman Munir, aged 19
(Daily Telegraph 6/12/02)

The Basic Teaching of Islam

"Whatever is just and good in other religions finds its deepest meaning and its final perfection in Christ."

Giulio Bassetti Sani

Islam was founded by a Saudi Arabian merchant, Muhamad al-Quraishi (570-632 AD). Islam is a religion based on a book - the Koran. Muslims believe that it was dictated verbatim to Muhamad (who is thought to have been illiterate (S7:158) over a period of 23 years. The Koran says that it came from an Eternal Tablet in heaven (S6:92; 43:3-4). It is to be accepted without question. The text is thought to have come initially by the Angel Gabriel (S2:97), also by other angels (S15:8), from the Holy Spirit (S26:192-194) and latterly by direct divine inspiration (S53:2-18).

The process from revelation to written form involved Muhamad remembering what he believed he had heard from God; at a later time Muhamad would recite the material to scribes who wrote it down on anything that came to hand. Several years later the fragments were collected and assembled - critics say with interference from the collators. It is difficult to know because any academic assessment of the Koran is forbidden. Unlike biblical criticism, it would be seen as blasphemy.

Photo Steve Bell©

Think of it like this...

The Koran teaches the existance of the Eternal Tablet, which has always existed in heaven. This seems to contradict the Islamic teaching that nothing lives with God in heaven - no son - nothing! Yet the Eternal Tablet is a direct parallel of the New Testament *'In the beginning the Word already existed. He was with God and He was God... So the Word became flesh and lived here on earth among us...' (John 1:1-2,14)* Jesus is the Eternal Tablet that was with God and came amongst men.

The Koran's 114 chapters (*suras*) are written in classical Arabic. This is the Semitic equivalent of William Shakespeare. The Koran, although not "inspired" in the biblical sense, cannot be less inspired than Shakespeare. The Muslim holy book's beauty and power impacts the Arabic speaker, regardless of the fact that many understand little of its classical language. The Koran is almost the length of the New Testament. Each chapter (*sura*) is arranged in order of length from the longest to the shortest. They are not chronological. The Koran was received in two cities - Mecca, the birthplace of Muhamad, and Medina where he fled under persecution.

The Basic Teaching of Islam

Meccan Suras (611-622 AD)

The Meccan Suras were received when Muslims were in the minority. On the whole, they are more diplomatic and philosophical and deal with issues similar to those of the minor prophets of the Old Testament. For example the call to worship one God, righteousness, justice, care for the poor and vulnerable. 'Meccan' Islam is the approach seen in the West.

Medinan Suras (623-632 AD)

The Medinan Suras were received when Muhamad was being resisted, though the Muslims were becoming the majority influence along the western coastal region of Arabia at that time. They are more assertive and violent, reflecting the politicised form of Islam we are familiar with today. 'Medinan' Islam is often enforced in the developing world.

The basic teaching of Islam is simple at the surface level, though the simplicity causes problems as you dig deeper. The language of Islam is Arabic, a 'root' language, which means that words are built up on a root structure. For example *s-l-m* is the root for the word *Islam* (submission to God). A *Muslim* (male) or *Muslima* (female) is someone who submits to God. The same root also gives us the word *salam* (peace).

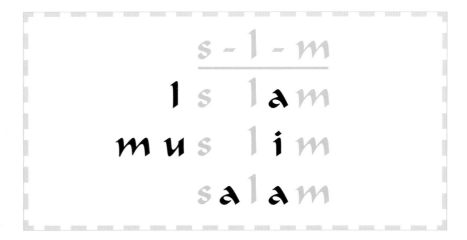

The Five Pillars (*Arkan al-Islam*) - The Muslim's practical duty (*din*)

Declaration of Faith (shahada)

Shahada is from the Arabic word for "certification", "testimony" or "witness". A shahid is a witness. This word is used to describe Muslim martyrs. The Shahada is the basic confession of Islam. It says "There is no god but Allah and Muhamad is His Messenger".

The Basic Teaching of Islam

Prayer (salat)

Muslim prayer is a debt and is supposed to be made five times a day as follows.

- *fajr* - dawn
- *zuhr* - mid-day
- *asr* - mid-afternoon
- *maghreb* - sunset
- *isha* - nightfall

Almsgiving (zakat, S2:271-273)

The prescribed alms to be given is 2.5% of the money left after routine bills are paid. Zakat is usually given for the maintenance of the local mosque or else direct to the poor.

Fasting (sawm, S2:183-187)

There are various annual fasts. Ramadan is the longest. A Muslim fast is from food, liquid, cigarettes and sexual intercourse between the hours of sunrise and sunset. The fasting Muslim will also try not to experience anything that might tempt their imagination. If they indulge in a wrong thing they count their fast as broken.

It is possible for Muslims to exempt themselves from fasting if they are a child, sick, travelling, or a pregnant woman or a nursing mother. Doctors often treat more people for stomach complaints during Ramadan than at any other time of the year. This is because after sunset, Islamic fasts are 'feasts' in the biblical sense.

Pilgrimage (hajj, S2:196-197)

All Muslims who are able-bodied are expected to make a pilgrimage to Mecca at least once in a lifetime. Pilgrims visit Mecca and Medina, the two cities associated with Muhamad's life. In Mecca they walk around the *ka'aba*. This is the edifice draped in black silk with Koranic verses carefully embroidered on it.

Many Muslims believe that all personal sin is forgiven on hajj and so Muslims will often wait until later on in their lives to make this expensive journey.

Struggle in the way of Islam (jihad)

This is not strictly a pillar of Islam at all. However, it is the principle underlying all the pillars and so is *de facto* the sixth pillar. Jihad is an Arabic word related to 'struggle'. Every effort should be made by the Muslim or Muslima (a female Muslim) to 'struggle' in the way of Islam by performing the five pillars. Jihad can also become violent struggle as was the case in the early days of Islam where 'holy war' was declared amongst the Arab tribes who were resistant to Islam. Political jihad has become prominent again over the past century as the oil boom has enabled certain Muslims to politicise Islam.

The Basic Teaching of Islam

3

Statistics:		(Newspaper headlines)
DEATH ON THE HAJJ		
1979	153 killed, 560 injured in a hostage incident	
1987	400 Iranians died in clashes with police	
1988	1 died and 16 injured in a bombing thought to be linked to Al-Qaeda	
1990	1,426 died of suffocation in a tunnel caused by a fire in Medina	
1991	200 Egyptian pilgrims drowned en route to Mecca when a ferry sank	
1994	270 pilgrims were killed in a stampede in Mecca	
1997	217 pilgrims were killed and 1,290 injured in a fire on the Mena plain where 70,000 tents caught fire, fanned by a strong breeze	

The Six Beliefs of Islam (Al-Iman) - The Muslim's faith

Allah (Tawhid, S37:35)

Muslims believe that God is one. The Arabic word *tawhid* means, 'oneness' or 'unity' i.e. of God. There are 99 'Most Beautiful Names', which are attributed to God. The Koran is clearer about what He is not rather than what He is. (S 112:1-4)

The Angels (Mala'ikatuhu, S35:1)

These include four archangels including Gabriel. Like the Bible, the Koran mentions an infinite number of ordinary angels. Muslims also believe in beings between the angels and humankind. These are called *jinn*, some of which are thought to be good, some evil and some neutral.

2

Photo courtesy of Frontiers International©

The Basic Teaching of Islam

The Books (Kutubuhu, S2:177)

Islam is a religion of up to 104 books. The word "bible" means 'library' and the Bible contains sixty-six books. Islam venerates only five of its books. All of them are believed to have originated in heaven on an 'Eternal Tablet'. They are understood to have been 'handed down' (*tanzil*) by revelation to different prophets at key points throughout history. The books are as follows…

* The Scrolls of Abraham (now lost)
* Tawrat by Moses - **Torah** i.e. the first five books of the Old Testament
* Zabur by David - **Psalms**
* Injil by Jesus - **Gospel**
* Qur'an by Muhamad - **Koran**
* Hadith - **Traditions** i.e. these are included but not strictly one of the books

Prophetic Messengers (Nabiim, S35:24)

Some Muslims believe there have been as many as 124,000 prophets. The Koran names about 25, 21 of whom are found in the Bible, for example Adam, Noah, Job, and John the Baptist. The top five 'messengers' of Islam are generally agreed as follows…

* Adam - **Adam** the first man
* Ibrahim - **Abraham** the first Muslim and the father of faith
* Musa - **Moses** the law-giver
* Isa - **Jesus** the Word of God
* Muhammed - **Muhamad** the last and greatest prophet

The Judgement (Yawm uddin S2:62)

This is the great day of recompense when good and bad deeds will be weighed in the divine balance. All people will be assigned either to Paradise or to Hell at the discretion of God. Some Muslims believe in a kind of purgatory, which is not taught in the Koran.

Allah's Decrees (Al-Qadar)

God's predestining of everything both good and evil. Fatalism is therefore a strong theme within the minds of Muslims who often hold to the idea of God as being capricious. Orthodox Islamic teaching seeks to hold a balance between the action of God and human responsibility.

The Basic Teaching of Islam

The Call to Prayer (athaan)

The following is the words 'intoned' by the Muezzin (the caller) from the minaret of the mosque.

Photo courtesy of Frontiers International ©

"God is most great. I bear witness that there is no god except God.

I bear witness that Muhamad is the Messenger of God.

Come to prayer.

Come to good.

Prayer is a better thing than sleep.

Come to the best deed.

God is most great. God is most great.

There is no god but God."

The First Sura of the Koran (fatiha)

The Arabic word *fatiha* comes from the word *fatah* (to open). This is the name given to the violent Palestinian resistance group. Al-Fatiha literally means 'the opening'. The following words form the opening sura of the Koran contains nothing an evangelical Christian would fundamentally disagree with.

The Fatiha

"In the Name of the merciful Lord of mercy.

Praise be to God, the Lord of all being,

The merciful Lord of mercy,

Master of the Day of Judgement.

Thee alone we worship

And to Thee alone we come for aid.

Guide us in the straight path,

The path of those whom You have blessed,

Not of those against whom there is displeasure, Nor of those who go astray."

Translation - Kenneth Cragg - The Event of the Qur'an page74

Why do Muslims follow Islam?

'Among the factors contributing to the rise of Islam was the failure of institutional Christianity in love, in purity, in fervour and in spirit. Islam therefore developed in an environment of imperfect Christianity… This is the tragedy of the rise of Islam, which claims to displace what it has never really known.'

Bishop Kenneth Cragg

Photo courtesy of Interserve ©

'20,000 Britons have converted to Islam over the past 20 years.'

(Daily Telegraph 6/02/02)

1slam is a huge global phenomenon. 1 in every 5 people on earth is a Muslim (i.e. 1.2 billion). If we believe in the sovereignty of God, the birth and growth of Islam cannot be a mistake. There must be a reason in the purposes of God who works everything out according to His own will and good pleasure.

There are several reasons why Muslims follow Islam. Here are some of them…

Muslims are born into Islam

Unlike the West, personal identity comes through being born Muslim. In a God-centred culture this is such a central feature that it can be more important than nationality. A Muslim also expects that someone born in Europe is a Christian. As a result, to the Muslim mind, Hitler was a Christian.

Islam is a culture

Islamic culture underlies every level of the Muslim's social network i.e. the nuclear family, the extended family and the wider clan. Islam is so intertwined with society that it rarely occurs to a Muslim to question this close-knit relational system. It is important to realise that Muslim culture is related to the biblical social-structure, which provides stronger cohesion than that of the West.

Many Muslims are nominal

A significant number of Muslims, particularly younger ones, find themselves born into Muslim families but are neither convinced nor practising Islam. For example a Turkish student said to me recently "I am not mu'min" (a true believer). There are many Muslims out there who pay lip-service to religious Islam but are, sometimes, very Westernised in their lifestyle and mindset.

Why do Muslims follow Islam?

Islam is a haven in a world of moral choices

One positive side to Islamic dogma is that Islam does give clear moral guidelines. A Muslim is instructed what to think and do from the moment they get out of bed to the moment they go to bed, and even what goes on while they are there. Some Muslims are clearly clinging tightly to Islam out of rejection of Western moral and spiritual values (or lack of them) and also materialism. Some Western converts to Islam to have life's decisions simplified and choices minimised.

Photo courtesy of AWM International©

'It is in the theology of history... that the deep causes of (Islam) must be sought'.

Msgr. Paul Mary Mulla

The Appeal of Islam

Islam carries a natural appeal to a variety of people for a number of reasons...

Developing World

- The appeal to some African societies, which practise 'traditional religion' is that Islam is the newest world religion. This can give novelty and the appearance that Islam is in some senses more up-to-date.

- Islam often appears to be culturally indigenous. This means it seems to be separated from anything Western in origin - unlike Christianity, which tends to be seen as a product of (if not a political tool of) the West.

- The non-Western persona of Islam is attractive in the post-colonial era. Of course in reality, Islam was born in the same part of the world as Christianity and into a similar culture. Islam was also involved in the slave trade of the colonial period. This is still going on today as young people are taken from Africa and Asia.

- The apparent worldwide brotherhood (*Umma*) of Muslims is attractive in poorer countries. In reality, there is a racial hierarchy with the Arabs being the first-class Muslims and African and Asian or Far Easterners as second and third-class Muslims.

The West

Western converts are often from the black communities of America and the UK. These people have suffered from racial discrimination and the lowest socio-economic

Why do Muslims follow Islam?

West

conditions in crime-ridden areas. The following are the top three reasons given to Jay Smith during research amongst American converts to Islam.

- Firstly Islam's social laws and the promise of order and stability is the most common reason for conversion. Islam is perceived to have the clout to deal with crime and injustice in society.

- Secondly, the unity of God (*tawhid*) is the next common reason. Islam offers a simple approach with no Trinity or intercessory mediator like Jesus. The Muslim is responsible for his or her own 'salvation'.

- Thirdly the notion of brotherhood. Islam endows the convert with a sense of the identity of God himself and the might of the house of Islam as a body of people. This is particularly attractive to the marginalised.

Other reasons for Western conversions to Islam include the apparent simplicity of Islam's teaching. The tenets of faith are simple and the practise of them is comparatively easy. Unlike Christianity, Islamic dogma is quantifiable so the Muslim knows how they have done. The tenets are to be accepted as written, without any interpretation or criticism. They are easily grasped and are palatable to the human mind. Islam does not require the revelation of the Holy Spirit to understand it, nor repentance nor a 'new birth' in order to live it.

Some Muslims will argue that the requirements of Islam are more reasonable and achievable (e.g. polygamy and easy divorce). For such Muslims, Islam is less hypocritical than Christianity, which attempts what they see as the impossible. Some Muslims also see Christianity as being professed in theory but abandoned in practise in the post-Christian West.

Arab

The Arab World

The heartlands of Islam include cultures, for which, image and 'saving face' is critical. We find that Islam, like Judaism, provides outward performance to which status is attached. For example during Ramadan in the Middle East the car I was being driven in, shunted a car parked outside a house. At the time the owner was sitting on his veranda dressed in an immaculately starched white *gallabiyya* (Arab gown) and white skull-cap. His fingers were 'telling' his prayer beads and he looked the picture of devout spirituality during the holiest month of the Islamic calendar. When he heard the crunch his piety instantly evaporated. He exploded into a fit of rage, grabbed an iron bar and hit our car then threatened to hit us too.

I see this incident, not so much as proof that Islam is somehow demonic, as a result of the fact that this poor man had just had his car dented on a hot day when he was in his best clothes and didn't want to have to deal with it. If we must talk demons, how does this incident compare with the 'road-rage' in the UK? I recently heard a public confession to such behaviour by a well-known Christian speaker who was making the point that we are all human.

Historic Barrier

Photo courtesy of AWM International ©

Barriers to the Gospel

When we first encounter a Muslim person it is understandable that they are viewing us viewing them. This is usually going on as we try to relate to each other through several barriers. These barriers stop us coming out onto the bridge of friendship. The barriers are held up by the A-E-I-O-U we mentioned in chapter one. They are *attitudinal* and *emotional* barriers, which persist, partly because we are starved of *information* about each other. We therefore avoid *opportunities*. Together all this creates the lack of *understanding* we are suffering from.

The barriers are the result of …

1. the negative interaction, which has happened between Christians and Muslims throughout history (i.e. the historical barrier)

2. the huge differences of worldview, values and lifestyle (i.e. the cultural barrier)

3. the sincere theological differences (i.e. the theological barrier)

4. and the terminology we use to speak about spiritual and moral issues (i.e. the communicational barrier).

These barriers are not insurmountable and Muslims are not always resistant to the efforts of Christians to overcome the barriers. However, to cross them does take a conscious effort on our part to 'think into the shoes' of a Muslim.

Historic Barriers

5

> 'St. Augustine of Hippo was one of the early Christians to define the Christian faith for the pagan mind, He ransacked secular thought for any points of communication so long as it didn't contradict the revealed truth of Scripture. 'The ancient Hebrew Tabernacle in the Wilderness was furnished by melting down the pagan statuettes and pharaonic jewellery of Egypt. The gold of Egypt is still gold! Wherever truth is to be found it is the Lord's.'
>
> *(Augustine)*

Historic barrier

One day on a university campus, an Iranian student was talking with a friend of mine, an American Christian. As the conversation headed towards spiritual issues the 'historical barrier' emerged for the Irani who began to get angry about the periods of history in which the West had bullied and damaged Muslim lands, leading to the actions of 11 September 2001. My American friend was taken aback by the fact that this young Muslim was actually hurting as a result of world events, which happened centuries before he was even born. My friend sincerely apologised and asked forgiveness on behalf of the perpetrators of past atrocities against Muslims in the name of Christ.

The atmosphere became static with tension as tears appeared in the eyes of the Irani Muslim who did not know how to handle such a demonstration of the spirit of Jesus. It was a 'grace response' on the part of the American.

So what exactly is it that provokes Islamic rage?

Photo Steve Bell ©

The Crusades (1096 - 1291AD)

A. The Crusades (1096 - 1291AD)

This episode of history is remembered in the Muslim World as though it happened last year. The Crusades were a series of jihad-like military operations undertaken by armies sanctioned by the Church and representing 'Christendom'. These military campaigns occurred over a period of time in which European armies of 'Christian' mercenaries marched across Europe to re-take Jerusalem from the occupying Arab Muslims. As part of these operations, soldiers indulged in indiscriminate rape, murder and unwarranted brutality.

It is also true to say that Islamic history features episodes of Muslim brutality to Muslim. Nevertheless, the Crusades are an era in Christian history, which the modern church must somehow own as misguided and sinful. We need to adopt a more humble attitude and move out in the genuine spirit of Jesus Christ to Muslims today.

Historic Barriers

'I remind you that during the Crusades, Muslims were attacked by Christians who came from Europe. 70,000 were killed in one day. Yet no Muslim authority has ever written against Christianity. We have always made a distinction between the religion and those who sully its name. In the case of September 11 you in the West did not make that distinction.'

Dr. Ahmad al-Tayyib
Grand Mufti of Al-Azhar
University, Cairo

A Muslim once remarked "You (Christians) do not love the Muslims. But then you do not love one another either. Just look at the way you are divided in many denominations and you are fighting one another in Ireland". This remark shows how Muslims assume two things.

First that if someone is born in Algeria they are automatically a Muslim and someone born in Europe is automatically a Christian. It may shock us to learn that, to the Muslim, the page three topless girls in the newspapers are all 'Christian'.

Second the Muslim assumes that, if in Islam, religion and state are the same thing, this must be true of the West i.e. Western politics is synonymous with Christianity.

B. The dismantling of the Ottoman Empire

The Ottoman Empire was the last vestige of Islamic greatness on the world stage. It went into decline as the amazing flowering of Islamic learning and culture began to disintegrate. This is a painful reality for many Muslims to accept. It was into this situation that the West intervened for a variety of reasons. This triggered, what appeared to be the carving up of the Empire by Western politicians almost over a cup of coffee in European capitals. Hence Saddam Hussein's claim to Kuwait was based on borders known in the region, which the West had moved to suit the political need of that day.

C. The establishing of the State of Israel

Britain, France and America were key players in the formation of the 'political state' of Israel. Reformist Muslims are anti-Israel rather than anti-Jewish per se - remember that Arabs themselves are Semites. The tension in the Middle East is like a family squabble between first cousins over rights to a piece of 'holy' land. It is an open question as to why the other Arab States are conspicuous by their absence in terms of trying to bring resolution or receive Palestinian exiles and refugees. It seems the Palestinian people are left as pawns in a wider political game. Colin Chapman's book *Whose Promised Land?* is an excellent overview of this situation - see Appendix 5.

Historic Barriers

5

> 'Israeli commandos do not cite the Hebrew prophet Joshua as they go into battle, but Muslim insurgents can readily invoke the example of their Prophet, Muhamad, who was a military commander himself. And while the Crusaders may have fought with the cross on their shields, they did not - could not - cite words from Jesus to justify their slaughter.'
>
> *Kenneth L Woodward (Newsweek, February 2002)*

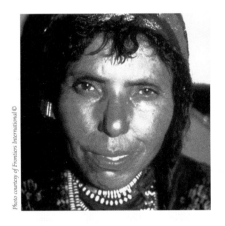

Photo courtesy of Frontiers International ©

Evangelical Christians often confuse the political state of Israel with the Israel of biblical prophecy. This leads to problems. For example…

• How far is the behaviour of the Israeli government towards Palestinian civilians worthy of the character of the God of Israel? How far can we call the more recent events the 'fulfilment of biblical prophecy'? For example John Pilger's documentary '*Palestine is still the Issue*' showed film footage of Israeli soldiers breaking the arms of Palestinian youths with boulders. In the same programme shown 15 September 2002 there were scenes where Israeli soldiers had defecated and fouled furniture, walls and equipment in every room as they ransacked Palestinian buildings, which were used for children and young people's social activities.

A male friend of mine applied as a volunteer on a kibbutz. Before being assigned a kibbutz he was told he would be posted according to his requirements i.e. did he want sex with girls, sex with boys or drugs. He would be assigned a placement accordingly.

• To what extent is the Old Testament injunction to care for the 'stranger in the midst' (Lev 19:18,33) being carried out? We must note the existence of significant human rights abuses, racism and an hedonistic and atheistic society in which Christian medical workers report that one free abortion is available to all serving female Israeli soldiers during their military service.

• Clearly one of the biggest blockages to gaining the trust of Muslims is the fact that they perceive the West (i.e. including the Christian Church), to be endorsing and financially supporting the political State of Israel. The American government aid package to Israel is several million dollars a day. However, there is a way to embrace the significance of Bible prophecy while standing up for biblical human rights and values with regard to the reality of Israel/Palestine and its peoples today.

The Gulf War

D. The Gulf War

This victory against Muslims by Muslims, with the help of non-Muslims, broke the understanding that God will never allow non-Muslims to triumph over Muslims in battle. The fact that this also happened centuries ago in Spain and again in Kuwait is a cause for understandable disquiet in the Muslim World.

Historic Barriers

5

E. Muslim World dependence on the West

Muslim economies need the West as the information provider and source of their technology to function in the modern world. Yet they despise the West's morality of convenience, godlessness, materialism, crime and violence. Many Muslims see the West as a sex-crazed, pornographic, perverted and lust-intoxicated culture.

F. Continued US presence in Saudi Arabia

Muslims see the continuing presence of American and allied forces (i.e. the *kufireen* or infidel) in Saudi as a continuation of the Crusades.

Photo courtesy of Interserve ©

G. Islamic structures in the modern world

Although Islam promises Muslims "the upper hand", their lands are often underdeveloped and disenfranchised compared to the "infidel" West. While this causes anger amongst hard-line Islamic groups, it begs the question as to why this should be the case. (see the quote by Dr Zaki Badawi on page 8).

The Cultural Barrier

Definitions of culture:

'Culture is an ordered way of life in which people do things together. It is any integrated system of learned behaviour patterns, characteristic of the members of a society, which are not the result of biological inheritance.'

Malinowski

'Culture is an integrated system of beliefs (i.e. God, reality or ultimate meaning), of values (i.e. what is true, good, beautiful or normative), of customs (i.e. how to behave, relate to others, talk, pray, dress, work, play, trade, farm, eat, etc), and of institutions which express these beliefs, values and customs (i.e government, law courts, temples or churches, family, schools, hospitals, factories, shops, unions, clubs, etc) which binds society together and gives it a sense of identity, dignity, security and continuity.'

Willowbank Report - Gospel & Culture, Lausanne Occasional Paper, No.2, Wheaton, 1978

The second barrier, which restricts relationship between people born into Muslim society and non-Muslims, is that of culture. Unlike the sacred/secular divide in Western culture, Islam blends itself into the life of its communities with almost seamless continuity. Islam becomes its own culture. Like Judaism, Islam is more than a religion, it is a way of life.

Culture is a complicated thing. Most people tend to spot surface issues when they are on package holidays. We identify things that are quaint but we can fail to recognise the deeper significance of culture, particularly our own. We now look at what culture is, how it impacts the way we decide what is "normal" and the pressing need to develop the skill of relating to people within other cultures.

Respect for culture:

Culture is a part of God's design for humankind. The positive creativity of culture is an important biblical value. Cultures are celebrated in heaven where tribes, languages and peoples are listed (Rev 5:9). The Apostle Paul, although often at

The Cultural Barrier

6

odds with his own race over the Gospel, was only too aware of his Jewish cultural roots. These affected him racially, educationally and spiritually (Phil 3:3-11). Culture could well be present in heaven as *'the kings of the earth bring their splendour into New Jerusalem'* (Rev 21:24). To relate to a Muslim with genuine respect for their culture will get us much further across the bridge of friendship than merely arguing doctrine. A Muslim is likely to notice what we are like, long before what we say. Our attitude will speak louder than our words. To get this wrong can lead to failure.

A girl on a mission in the north of England accosted an elderly Muslim outside a public convenience. It was summer time and she was wearing a skimpy tightly fitting vest and tight shorts. She shoved a tract at the Muslim and said "Jesus is the Son of God and died for your sins, if you repent and accept him into your life as your personal Saviour you can go to heaven". The Muslim was furious. She was devastated and tearfully reported back to her group how hard Muslims are to evangelise. In reality she had broken every cultural rule in the book and had offended the Muslim and left him further away from the gospel than when she started.

'There are strengths and weaknesses, which normally come bundled up together. Thus people in the West tend to admire, rather guiltily, the concern (Muslims) show for the elderly, while being critical of the pressure on young people to conform to arranged marriages…both have a common root in respect for elders…'

J & S Root

Western cultures are no better or worse than Muslim cultures - just different. It is interesting how Western society affirms other cultures in line with political correctness, while reacting judgementally to issues like female circumcision and arranged marriages.

'Because man is God's creation, some of his culture is rich in beauty and goodness. Because man is fallen, all of his culture is tainted with sin - some of it is demonic.'

The key issue is to look for the open doors for the Gospel in the other culture. An excellent example of this is the Apostle Paul in Athens (Acts 17). He gave a superb cross-cultural open-air message, which maximised his access to the 'open doors' in their thinking while minimising the possibility of misunderstanding.

One way to understand the illusive concept of culture is to ask what comes into your mind when you think of - for example - the idea of being French e.g. The Eiffel Tower, baguettes, onions, good wine, the French language and the war time French Resistance. Of course these are only surface stereotypes, which are a caricature of real French culture, but it is a start.

Cement is made up of natural ingredients but its use is cultural
e.g. a pavement or a minaret.
Cotton is natural but its use is cultural e.g. pin-striped shirts or a sari.

The Cultural Barrier

6

Now what comes to your mind when you think of being British? e.g. Bag Pipes, Morris dancing, monarchy, the last night of the Proms, candy floss, Pearly Queens, Fish & Chips and quaint country villages. The list of such cultural 'icons' is endless but they are still only surface observations. When we recognise how shallow these images are, we realise how much we tend to charicature Muslim cultures. This can be as unhelpful to them as it is to us. The inevitable contrast between cultures can become a clash if we are not careful. Here are some contrasts to look out for in Muslim cultures. Just ask yourself what are the implications of each. Which are more biblical?

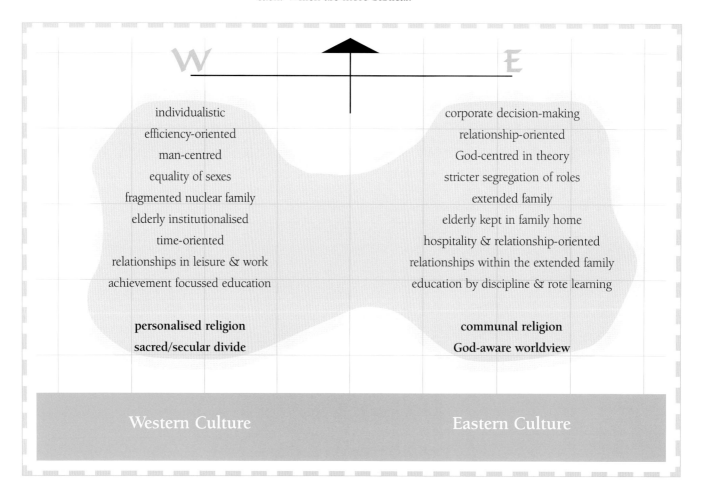

Western Culture	Eastern Culture
individualistic	corporate decision-making
efficiency-oriented	relationship-oriented
man-centred	God-centred in theory
equality of sexes	stricter segregation of roles
fragmented nuclear family	extended family
elderly institutionalised	elderly kept in family home
time-oriented	hospitality & relationship-oriented
relationships in leisure & work	relationships within the extended family
achievement focussed education	education by discipline & rote learning
personalised religion	**communal religion**
sacred/secular divide	**God-aware worldview**

How can I define my own culture?

It is always hardest to define your own culture. This is made harder because of the effect of 'globalisation', which is causing even traditional cultures to change rapidly and merge together with increasing inter-connectedness. However, one way to identify your own culture at work is to ask questions like…

* Is it 'the done thing' to talk to people on public transport - if not why not? If it is, what topics are appropriate - why?

* As a teenager, what weight were you expected to give to your parents' authority - why?

* What sort of relating is acceptable between unmarried people of the opposite gender - why?

The Cultural Barrier

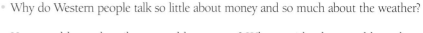

- Why do Western people talk so little about money and so much about the weather?

- How would you describe your table manners? Where, with whom and how do you eat i.e. what utensils do you use? - why?

- How do you spend your leisure time - why?

- Which relationships are most important to you - why?

- How do you prefer to communicate over distances - why?

- What is your feeling about punctuality? - why?

- Is queuing important to you - If so why? If not, why not?

- Why do you say "Fine!" when asked "How are you?"?

How can I get a handle on Muslim cultures?

We said earlier that Muslim cultures are many and varied around the world. Muslims can be as foreign to each other as Europeans, Australians and Americans. Like Europeans, Muslims are divided by their different languages, traditional dress, food, history and general way of life. Muslim cultures are often partly biblical because Islam was born in the same broad cultural context as the Old Testament.

Here are some aspects of Muslim culture, which are common to many societies and are found in the West, particularly amongst the older generation or those who have arrived more recently and are therefore less culturally integrated.

- Indirect negotiation i.e. talking round the houses before coming to the point - see Genesis 23

- Respect for elders and old age - see Leviticus 19:32

- Segregation of genders

- Extended family with male priority - grand father, father, oldest son, then mother

- Lofty concept of God - see Exodus 34:1-8

- Modesty of dress - males cover naval to knee, females from neck to wrist and ankle.

- Modesty of behaviour - Matthew 5:27

- Official abstinence from alcohol and pork

- God-centred mind-set

- Respect for religious observance - see Matthew 5:17-20; 6:1-6

- Religion as a topic of conversation

- Religious phraseology - see John 20:26

- Corporate consciousness - little privacy or individual decision-making

- Family and relationship-oriented networks

Photo courtesy of Frontiers International ©

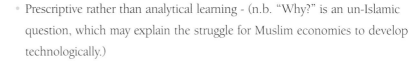

The Cultural Barrier

6

'Islam is both religion and lifestyle'

Muslim proverb

- Prescriptive rather than analytical learning - (n.b. "Why?" is an un-Islamic question, which may explain the struggle for Muslim economies to develop technologically.)

- Saving of 'face' or dignity - not to be belittled in front of others

- Supernatural and magical awareness with natural/spiritual continuum

- Leisure time is family-oriented

- Accepting of 'fate' as God's will - greater resignation to circumstances

- The traditional payment of dowry usually paid in jewellery is still practised

Cross-cultural do's and don'ts

The following points are aimed at relating to older, conservative and more devout Muslims. Many of the points may not actually be a problem, even to such Muslims, so rather than assuming, either be sensitive or, if in doubt, just ask.

Most of the points are totally irrelevant for younger, more Westernised Muslims whose values will be a mix of both Muslim and Western culture.

Don't

1. Don't try to compliment or criticise Muhamad or Islam - be tactful but honest.

2. Don't refer to the Koran as poetry. In Islam poets are generally thought to be demon-inspired.

3. Don't play music (especially modern Gospel) if your Muslim friend is devout as music is seen as associated with immorality in Islam. Remember neither music nor singing is part of Muslim worship. Chanting is not seen as singing.

4. Don't use your left hand to eat with or pass food to a devout Muslim. The left hand is taboo as it is the 'toilet' hand in many Muslim cultures.

5. Don't offer alcohol, pork, pork products or anything made from animal oils. All these break the *halal* law of Islam.

6. Don't point the sole of your stocking foot or shoe at a Muslim. This is insulting.

7. Don't tell jokes unless you know your Muslim friend really well. Jokes often backfire cross-culturally and can lead to misunderstanding.

8. Don't ask about the spouse of your Muslim friend as this can be taken to be odd and intrusive. It is better to ask generally "How is the family?".

9. Don't try to talk to a Muslim while they are eating unless they initiate it. Muslims tend to eat first and talk later.

10. Don't ask to use the toilet in a Muslim's home if at all possible. As with Gentiles to Jews, non-Muslims present an uncertainty in the area of ritual hygiene.

11. Don't mishandle the Bible or Koran by putting either of them on the floor if at all possible. Muslims normally keep them wrapped up and in a high place.

12. Don't write or underline the Bible or Koran you use to discuss with your friend.

The Cultural Barrier

6

13. Don't compliment a devout Muslim parent on the looks or abilities of their child. They may believe that this will attract the attention of the 'evil eye' through envy.

14. Don't discuss religion near an unclean place e.g. rubbish or toilet.

15. Don't say anything, which is openly supportive of the political state of Israel. It is better to refer to it as Palestine.

16. Don't smile and laugh with people of the opposite gender.

17. Don't point directly at someone if you can help it.

18. Don't assume you know what a Muslim believes - always ask.

Do ▶

1. Do greet junior people first and acknowledge everyone in a room.

2. Do shake hands with people but don't linger with people of the opposite gender. A Muslim proverb says '*Guilt slips away through the hands*'. The greeting carries a social function of establishing peace in your relationship even when there has been misunderstanding.

3. Do take time to ask after "the family" in detail.

4. Do be ready to be embraced by an Asian or kissed on both cheeks by an Arab. Arabs also may linger holding your hand long after shaking it.

5. Do remove your shoes in the home of a devout Muslim. Wear clean socks.

6. Do sit with people of your own gender. The seat nearest the door is the humblest place. You may be invited to a more prominent chair (Luke 14:10).

7. Do sit with good, if slightly formal, posture and keep your feet on the floor as opposed to slouching.

8. Do use both hands to offer anything. To use one hand communicates half-heartedness and lack of respect for the person.

9. Do be objective about the moral failings of your own nation and express interest in their perceptions of it.

10. Do avert your eyes from staring into the eyes of a Muslim of the opposite gender. Too much eye contact is seen as forward and flirtatious.

11. Do try to remember to enter a room right foot first as this may be the custom of your friend.

Photo courtesy of Frontiers International ©

12. Do excuse yourself to go and wash your hands before handling a Bible or Koran. Always hold either book in the right hand to show respect for it and carry in a covering.

13. Do remove any statues, crosses or Jewish six-pointed stars from your home or jewellery in the presence of a devout Muslim.

14. Do lock your dog away and remove their food bowls etc. Dogs are seen by devout Muslims as unclean.

The Theological Barrier

"All fundamental differences between Islam and Christianity are rooted in the perception of God. Islam perceives God to be a being who does not seek relationship and is unknowable while Christianity perceives God to be a person who came into Eden calling for man. He has been actively seeking relationship with people ever since."

Jay Smith (adapted)

Muslims are not Jehovah's Witnesses. This is to say that doctrine is not the prime concern when we first try to form friendship with a Muslim. The problem is not primarily the conflict of doctrines but the clash of worldviews. The Muslim worldview is based on a clear and prescriptive belief system while the Western worldview has increasingly moved away from its moral and spiritual foundations in the Judeo-Christian heritage of the Bible.

This difference of perspective on life gives rise to huge misunderstandings. As someone once put it, the problem is not two groups of people who are separated on the same planet, but rather it is two groups of people co-existing side by side while living on different planets.

Photo Steve Bell ©

"Like many Westerners who have never held a Koran but still have definite views about it, your Muslim friend may have never seen the Bible in their own language but will likely have all sorts of opinions about it."

Having said all that, we do eventually have to face the fact that the contrasts between Islamic and Christian doctrine are significant and have to be faced up to. If we cannot overcome the first three barriers, we will probably never earn the right, in a Muslim's eyes, to address the fourth. What follows is a comparison of Islamic and biblical teaching on a variety of issues.

The Theological Barrier

7

MUSLIM BELIEFS	CHRISTIAN BELIEFS
Religion for God 'If anyone desires a *religion* other than Islam, it shall not be accepted from him and in the world to come he shall surely be among the losers'. (S3:85) n.b. Muhamad is a bringer of religion.	**Relationship with God** '…neither is *salvation* in any other, for there is no other name under heaven given among men by which we must be saved'. n.b. Jesus came to bring, not religion but salvation (Acts 4:12)
Identity of Allah There is only one High God of the universe who is worshipped inadequately by Jews and Christians alike. '*Our God and your God is One*'. (S 29:46; 3:64) See '*Allah - God of the Bible?*' in '*Appendix 6*'.	**Identity of Allah** Although controversial among Christians, the name *Allah* comes from *El-illah*. This means *High God* and was known in the Middle East long before Islam. Linguistically Allah is related to the Hebrew version *El* of the Old Testament (e.g. El-ohim, El-Shaddai). Allah is the only word available to millions of Arabic speaking Christians. Allah is the God of the Bible with the proviso that Muslims' understanding of Him is faulty.
Inspiration of Scripture The very words of the Koran were revealed to Muhammad. He simply received them like a typewriter and recited them to scribes. His thought and ideas were not involved (S29:48) It is unnecessary and wrong to examine the "sources" of the Koran. Because the Koran was received in Arabic it must be recited and read in Arabic. Translations are not valued and only regarded as giving the general meaning.	**Inspiration of Scripture** The writers of the Bible were inspired by the Holy Spirit (1 Pet 1:21). It shows the individual personality of the writers. In this sense the Bible is the Word of God and entrusted through men. Although the Bible writers were inspired, we are encouraged to compare and search the Scriptures. The OT was written in Hebrew and Aramaic, the NT in Greek. A translation of the Bible is just as much the Bible as the Hebrew original. The point is intelligibility of the truth not veneration of the text.
The Eternal Tablet The verbal revelations of Torah, Psalms, Gospel and Koran come from a template in heaven (S85:22). This is also called 'The Mother of the Book' (S3:7; 13:39; 43:4).	**The Eternal Tablet** Jesus is the dynamic equivalent of the Eternal Tablet. He is the Word of God who was with God from eternity (John 1:1-2; Hebrews 1:1). Islam teaches that nothing dwells with God, but the Eternal Tablet contradicts that.

The Theological Barrier

MUSLIM BELIEFS	CHRISTIAN BELIEFS
Transcendence & Sovereignty of God God is greater than all our ideas about Him. He is Lord of the Worlds (S1), the Creator and Sustainer of the universe (S3:189). At the same time he is nearer to man than his jugular vein (S50:16). God is almighty and predestines everything in the universe, including both good and evil.	**Transcendence & Sovereignty of God** Christians have a similar belief in God's sovereignty but stress God's nearness ('The Kingdom of God is at hand'). God is available to all of us in Christ. Christians try to keep the balance between God's sovereignty and man's free will and responsibility. However less stress is put on the idea of God's determining of everything and almost none on God decreeing evil.
Man as a creature The relationship of man to God is as a servant to his Master.	**Man as a creature** Man was created in the "image and likeness of God" (Gen 1:27). This image is spoiled but not destroyed. God reached out to make us his children in Christ. We believe that man was created to 'tend the earth and subdue it' (Gen 1:28).
Man as a sinner When Adam sinned, it was personal to him. It did not amount to a "Fall" for the whole human race. Everyone is born sinless with a clean sheet before God. Sin is a fault (S4:111; 6:120; 24:11). We must try harder if we sin.	**Man as a sinner** Adam's sin affected the whole human race (Ps 51:5; Rom 3:23; 5:12; 1 Cor 15:22). Original sin means we inherit a fallen human nature from our parents. We sin because we are sinners. We are born in alienation from God and need reconciling back into relationship with him.
The Law of God God's requirements are contained in the law (shari'a) and the most important are the Five Pillars of Islam.	**The Law of God** God's basic requirements are revealed in the 10 Commandments, which cover our relationship to God and our neighbours.
Creation of the world Mankind was created in Paradise (janna). He was banished to earth (S2:36). Various numbers of days are given for the creation. A cluster of days is also mentioned. This allows for a 'day' being millions of years and therefore it is sufficiently vague as to be compatible with evolution theory. Man was created carnivorous and cattle were created for man to eat (S6:142; 16;5). Adam & Eve became aware that they were naked after they sinned (S20:121). The Koran also suggests they were clothed before the fall (S7:27).	**Creation of the world** Mankind was created on earth in the Garden of Eden. (Gen 2:8) and later banished from it. However we understand the "days" of Genesis, the earth came before the Sun, which may rule out a 'big bang'. Man and animals were created vegetarian (Gen 1:29-30). Originally there was no death and suffering. Mankind was created naked and not ashamed (Gen 2:25). Shame came with sin.

The Theological Barrier

7

MUSLIM BELIEFS	CHRISTIAN BELIEFS
Salvation Only by submission to God and Koran can we escape the 'Blazing Fire' (S3:85). Salvation is by *falah* (self-effort or positive achievement) (S23:102-103).	**Salvation** This is only possible through Jesus Christ (Jn 14:6; Acts 4:12). It is by grace through faith (Eph 2:8-9)
Mission Spreading Islam is called *dahwa* (invitation). This may be by many methods i.e. educational, cultural, community development or by force where necessary.	**Mission** Spreading of the Gospel is with gentleness (Lk 10:3,36-37) and respect (1 Pt 3:15). No earthly weaponry is used (2 Cor 10:3-5) and the response is voluntary.
The Fall of Man Satan enticed Adam and Eve (S7:20-21; 20:120). The 'mistake' only affected Adam. Man is not a sinner, just weak (S4:28) and rebellious (S96:6). The couple were given 'raiment' but no mention of this being skins (S7:26). Work, sweat and struggle were part of the original creation order (S90:4). Death is not an enemy it is part of the original created order.	**The Fall of Man** The serpent enticed Eve, denying she would die (Gen 3:1-5). Adam's sin somehow entered the bloodline and gene pool. All are now born with the sin principle in them. God provided garments of skins (Gen 3:21). 'Painful toil' and sweat are a product of the curse (Gen 3:17,19). Death is an enemy resulting from the fall of man (Gen 2:17; 3:19; Rom 5:12; 17:1; 1 Cor 15:21-22,26).
Flesh/spirit struggle Compromise with sensual and physical aspects of life.	**Flesh/spirit struggle** We struggle against the flesh (Rom 5-8; Gals 5:16). Some Christians fail.

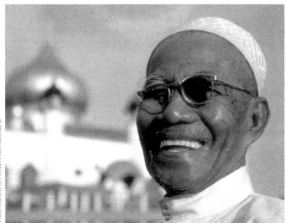

Photo courtesy of Frontiers International©

The Shahada or Islamic creed -
"There is no god but God and Muhamad is the apostle of God"

The Theological Barrier

7

Supremacy of Muhamad over Christ

As the final and universal prophet, Muhamad is seen as superior to all others, including Jesus Christ whom Muslims think is only a prophet to the Jews (S3:49; Isaiah 49:6).

Muhamad is called the 'unlettered one' and is seen as the fulfilment of Messianic prophecies.

Bible texts used by Muslims to refer to Muhamad include …

- Gen 17:20 - one from Ishmael's house is taken to be a reference to Muhamad
- Deut 33:2 - is seen as reference to Arabs
- Ps 45 - is seen as ode to Muhamad
- Ps149:6-9 - is seen as Islamic conquest
- Isaiah 42:1-4; 53; 63:1-6; Hag 2:7; Mat 3:3; 21:43-44; Mk1:7 are seen as references to Muhamad.
- Jn 4:21; Jude 14:15 - are seen as reference to Islam.

Muhamad was a sinner (S40:55;47:19;48:2;94:1-3).

The Holy Spirit

The Koran mentions the Holy Spirit (S2:87; 17:85; 70:4; 78:38; 97:4). However Muslims see Him as Gabriel or the act of revelation (S16:102; 42:52). Another text used is Jn 14:16,17,26 - *Parakletos* (comforter) which is claimed to be a reference to Muhamad. Muslim tradition teaches that Christians changed the text from *Parakultos*, which is the equivalent of *ahmad* (the praised one), the Arabic root of the name *Muhamad* (S61:6).

Supremacy of Qur'an over the Bible

The Koran teaches respect for the Sciptures (S3:84; 4:136) but Muslims' have an 'abstract' respect for Torah and Injil as they believe the Koran contains the truth more perfectly. Yet the Koran persistently misquotes the Bible.
For example…

- Abraham's father was not Azar as in S6:74, but Terah (Gen 11:26).
- Pharaoh's daughter, not his wife, adopted Moses as in S28:7-9 (see Ex 2:5-20).
- Aaron's sister Miriam was not Mary the mother of Jesus as in S19:27-28. (see Ex 15:20 and Num 26-59).
- Pharaoh did not instruct Haman to build the Tower of Babel as in Sura 28:38. It happened in Babylon generations earlier (Gen 11:1-9).
- Joseph did not have his shirt torn by Potipher's wife as in S12:23-29. He fled the temptation (Genesis 39:9-12)

Supremacy of Christ over Muhammed

Biblical prophecy consistently points to a Jew as the one who was to come. For example Gen 49:10 shows that the obedience of the nations was to be to one from the house of Judah. Christians believe that the references opposite have been lifted and reapplied to Muhamad, who came after Jesus, the One they really refer to.

Everything was created through Christ, who was pre-existent before creation (Gen 1:26; 3:22; 11:7; Mic 5:2; Jn 1:1-3, 10; 3:13; 6:62; 8:35,58; 17:5, 24; Rom 11:36; 1 Cor 8:6; Cols 1:16-17; Heb 1:2)

Jesus is the Messiah of the Old Testament (Is 7:14 & Mat 1:22-23; Mic 5:2 & Mat 2:1-6; Is 61:1-2 & Lk 4:16-21; Is 52:13 & Ac 8:29-35; Ps 16:8-11 & Ac 2:22-36). There is no biblical support for Muhamad's work.

Jesus is never referred to as a sinner in the Koran. He is the 'Holy son' (S19:19).

The Holy Spirit

From earliest church history has come the definitive statement 'I believe in the Holy Spirit, the Lord and giver of life, who proceeds from the Father and the Son; who together with them is worshipped and glorified' (Nicene Creed).

See Gen 1:2; Rom 8; Eph 4:30; 1 Cor 6:19. The Holy Spirit is personal, active and involved in God's world.

Supremacy of Bible over Qur'an

Some Muslims see the Old and New Covenants as contradictory e.g. '*An eye for an eye and a tooth for a tooth*' in contrast to '*Love your enemies*'. The Bible is a 'developmental' revelation through history. However, the Koran does contradict itself. For example.

- God will never forgive associating a partner with Him (S4:116), yet Abraham did this very thing (S6:76-78).
- The Koran claims to confirm both Tawrat & Injil (S3:3) yet it appears to contradict the central doctrines e.g. Jesus' divine nature, the Cross, His atonement for sin, and His resurrection.
- The Koran denies the crucifixion in S4:157-158, then seems to affirm it (S3:55).
- The Koran is positive about Christians (S29:46) as well as negative (S5:54)
- The Koran says creation took 6 days (S25:59) then 8 days (S41:9-12).

 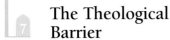

The Theological Barrier

MUSLIM OBJECTIONS to the Gospel

The Person of Christ

Jesus is a revered prophet of Islam. He is seen as a created being (S3:59) and a prophet to the Jews. He was born of a virgin (S19:19-21). He was superior to all other men (S66:12). He is *Kalimat Allah* (Word of God), *Ruhallah* (Spirit of God) (S4:171) *Kalimat ul-haq* (Word of Truth) (S19:34) and *Qudoos* (Holy) (S19:19). He is known by Muslims as *The miracle working prophet* (S3:49).

Muhamad was committed to correcting distorted Jewish and early Christian error about Jesus. 'If the All-merciful has a son, then I am the first to serve him' (S43:81). (See Appendix 1 page 71.)

The Corruption of the Bible

The Koran is the revelation of God's will. It is the final, pure and verbatim word of God. The Bible allows for human personality and therefore error. An Islamic tradition says that it has been tampered with and changed (S2:59; 7:162). This concept of "corruption" is called *tahrif*, which comes from *harrafa* in Arabic.

Nowhere does the Koran actually say that *tahrif* applies to the Bible (S4:46). Rather than stating that the Bible has been changed, the accusation in this verse was that certain Jews misrepresented their own Scripture and also Muhamad's words (S2:75).

The 'Gospel of Barnabas' was written in the 16th Century by an Italian convert to Islam. It was later discovered in Amsterdam in 1709 and this is hailed by some Muslims as the true *Injil* (Gospel). It supports the Muslim objection about Jesus' deity, death and the Trinity. It has serious errors of history and geography and it even contradicts the Koran. (See page 73.)

Muslims believe the Bible is now *mansukh* (redundant or superseded) by the Koran.

Four Gospels

Why do Christians have four Gospels today when there was only one true Gospel? This is evidence of additions by the church.

CHRISTIAN RESPONSES to Muslim objections

The Person of Christ

Jesus himself claimed the title 'Son of God' (Mat 2:11; 16:13-17; Mk 5:6-7 Jn 1:1; 9:35-38;11:4; 20:28). "Son of God" refers to Jesus' perfect humanity more than his divinity. The "I Am" titles speak more of His divinity.

'Son of'… is a Middle Eastern phrase showing an inseparable connection e.g. Barnabas (son of encouragement). Muhamad was none of the things listed opposite. (See also Psalm 2; 22 & 24). The tradition that Jesus is "only" an apostle is based on the Arabic expression '*inna maa*'. This can be translated either "only" or "certainly". Muhamad's insistence was probably that Jesus was "certainly" an apostle of God. This was probably aimed at convincing Jews who rejected Jesus altogether. It makes no sense for him to say to the Jews that Jesus is "only" a prophet.

The Integrity of the Bible

The Bible is the revelation of God Himself. Its inspiration is not verbatim but truth poured through human personalities.

Muslims should believe the Tawrat and Injil (S2:136;4:136). The Koran confirms them (S10:37; 35:31). Any words of God cannot be changed by men (S6:34; 10:64).

- When was the Bible changed?
  It could not have been before 622 AD as the Koran affirms that the Bible was the accurate Word of God at that date (S2:136; 4:136). The earliest biblical manuscripts in the British Museum date from before Muhamad; there is no change. If God preserved the Koran for 1,400 years from corruption, why could he not also preserve the Bible, which the Koran affirms as being protected by God?
- Where was the Bible changed?
  Hundreds of manuscripts in a dozen ancient languages have existed since before 622 AD. All agree with current manuscripts. No one could have altered all the originals in the world and then made our modern translation the same corrupted version.
- Who changed it?
  Why would Jews or Christians want to change the Bible?
- Why did God not permit Muslim scholars to save the original? Nowhere does the Koran state this; in fact it states the opposite (S10:64).

Four Gospels

God used individual personalities. The four Gospels are differing perspectives of Jesus Christ who is the one Gospel. This is integral to the truth expressed through them.

The Theological Barrier

7

The Trinity

The Islamic view of God is governed by the concept of *tawhid* (the unity of God i.e. *"Allah il-waheed"* - God is one).

Some Muslims may even think that Christians believe in three gods (i.e. God the Father, Mary the Mother and Jesus their offspring son by a physical relationship) (S9:30-31). This impression is strengthened by the traditional Roman Catholic image of the Madonna and Child. This is *shirk* (putting something on an equal level to God i.e. idolatry).

Gabriel's announcement to Mary is taken by some Muslims to be a sexual description i.e. *"The Holy Spirit will come upon you and the power of the Highest shall overshadow you and the thing to be born of you shall be called the Son of God"* (Luke 1:31).

(n.b. The three speakers in the Koran are God, the angel and Muhamad. Where God is speaking, He mostly uses the first person plural expression "We". Some scholars believe this is not the 'royal we' but came from the OT Scriptures which Muhamad may have been drawing on in "preparation" of the Arabs for the mystery of the Trinity.)

The Crucifixion

Muslims do not expect suffering for Jesus as an esteemed prophet of Islam. The Cross is therefore seen as an insult to the Islamic assumption of honour, power and prestige.

A Muslim tradition says that Judas died in Jesus' place and was made by God to look like Jesus. *'They killed him not nor crucified him, but so it was made to appear...Allah raised him to himself'.* (S4:157-158). The Koran does however, refer to Jesus as the Lamb of God (S3:39) in agreement with John 1:29. It also agrees with the sacrifice of Abraham's son (S 37:107), though tradition says it was Ishmael not Isaac. This is celebrated as Eid Al-Adha (Sheep Feast), also called Eid Al-Kibir. This is atonement by blood as found in Num 19:1-10.

The Trinity

The 'oneness' of God is biblical. 'Hear O Israel, the Lord our Lord is one Lord' (Deut 6:4). See also Gen 1:25, Deut 4:32.

Christians agree that it is blasphemous to suggest that God physically sired Jesus. The Trinity is not three gods but one God revealed in three persons. Jesus was the Word of God from all eternity, but became God's son at Bethlehem (Hebs 1:5-6). Muslims argue that if God gained a son it would be supernaturally. n.b. It was!

The Trinity is revealed throughout the Bible. It is not the invention of Christians. The concept is grasped by revelation not intellect, though the following illustrations might help.

The godhead is more like a family firm of three directors. The Trinity poses the idea of multiplication i.e. $1 \times 1 \times 1 = 1$ rather than addition i.e. $1 + 1 + 1 = 3$. The following illustrations are not really biblical and less helpful to Westerners, let alone Muslims.

- A man can be a trinity of father, son & husband in one
- The human being is a trinity of spirit, soul & body
- Water comes in three forms - liquid, solid (ice) or steam
- An egg is a trinity of yoke, white & shell

The Crucifixion

If Muhamad suffered, then a prophet of Islam can suffer. (See the Bill Musk quote page 62).

If God put someone else on the Cross instead of Jesus it would be a deception, which would be a violation of His character.

S19:32-34 says God took Jesus directly to heaven and that he will return to die and be raised to life again. The Koran contradicts this in S4:158 where it says God "caused" Jesus to die (Arabic: *mutawafiq*) and raised him to life again - ie. according to the Gospels.

Biblical prophecies and Jesus' own predictions specify that it would be Him who would die on the Cross (see Is 52: 13-53:12; Ps 22; Matt 20:17-19; 26:2,28,31-32,56; Lk 23:33; Jn 20:27; Cols 1:22; 1 Pet 1:18-19; Heb 9:13-14).

Think of it like this...

The parallel of Jesus in Islam is not Muhammed but the Qur'an (i.e. the Koran is the 'word' made book while Jesus is the Word made flesh).

The parallel of Muhammed in Christianity is not Jesus but Mary (i.e. both Muslims and Christians see these two as carrying the 'word of God' into the world).

The Theological Barrier

7

What Islam denies Muslims

1. The truth of original sin	It becomes "human weakness" or "mistakes" to be corrected.
2. The availability of grace	In Islam God has no desire for relationship. There is only *taqdir* (predetermination). Man lives negotiating with God in the hope of doing better in future.
3. Repentance	They can only hope for self-improvement.
4. Personal forgiveness	There is no heart cleansing, only ritual purity. God may act with clemency on Judgement Day or He may not.
5. Salvation	Only God coming to your help in the pressures of life like the deliverances sung about by the Psalmist David.
6. Relationship with God	Only fear and awe towards a distant God.
7. The New Birth	Muslims see no need, so this remains a redundant concept.
8. Assurance of heaven	Only fearful awaiting Judgement Day hoping all will be well. Heaven is the sensuous abode of men (S46:9).
9. Covenant-keeping God	Only an arbitrary God who is unpredictable.

Think of it like this...

'The Black Stone'

The Ka'aba is built on a rock formation, which has a black chunk of meteorite stone built into one corner. This is worn smooth, which has given rise to the tradition that this is the result of centuries of kissing and touching by Muslim pilgrims. Jesus is the cornerstone of the church (Eph 2:20). He is therefore the equivalent 'Black Stone' of the Christian faith. The Bible encourages worshippers of God to venerate Him when it says *'Kiss the Son so He will not be angry with you…'* (Psalm 2).

'As a prophet rejected by his own people, the Qur'anic Jesus (Isa) looks a lot like Muhamad, who was at first rejected by the people of Mecca'.

Kenneth L. Woodward

Christ in the Koran

(Acknowledgement - *Carey College* Booklet Series)

The Koran can become a stepping-stone to the truth of Christ for enquiring Muslims. This is possible because there are significant details about Jesus in the Koran. He is repeatedly referred to as "*Isa ibn Miryam*" (Jesus son of Mary). Muhamad seemed to defend Jesus against the Jewish insistence that he was illegitimate.

7 The Theological Barrier

'That is our argument which we bestowed upon Abraham as against his people. We raise up in degrees whom We will; Surely your Lord is All-wise, All-knowing. And We gave to him Isaac & Jacob And Noah We guided before and his seed David & Solomon, Job & Joseph Moses & Aaron - Even so we recompense the good-doers - Zachariah & Yehya, JESUS & Elijah; Each was of the righteous; Ishmael & Elisha, Jonah & Lot Each one We preferred before all beings.'

(S6:83-86)

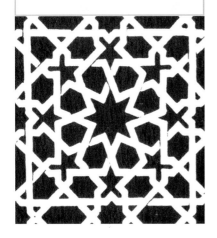

Jesus is also given an eminent position in the Koran. He is even superior to Muhamad himself. Jesus' supernatural character and holiness are made clear. Anyone insulting Jesus or Mary is warned (S4:155-156). One example of the high honour given to Jesus in the Koran is as follows…

Kenneth Cragg draws our attention to what he sees as Jesus being a diadem set in a tiara of prophetic jewels. For example Old Testament characters like Abraham are listed as 'types' of the Messiah. Isaac and Jacob, David and Solomon are types of the **kingly Christ**. Job and Joseph are types of the **suffering Christ**, while Moses and Aaron are types of the law-giving and **high priestly Christ**. The New Testament names Zachariah and Yehya (John Baptist) were respectively the 'announcer' and 'witness' to the **arrival of Christ**. Elijah (1 Kgs 17:17-24), Ishmael (Gen 21:14-19), and Elisha (2 Kgs 4:32-37) are all types of the **resurrected Christ**.

All this can help a Muslim enquirer go through the stepping-stone effect by pressing on from the Koran into the Bible to find the answers to the questions the Koran poses about Jesus.

There is enough material about Jesus in the Koran to lead a Muslim enquirer well on their way to faith in Him. When you are reading the Bible with a Muslim friend it is helpful to look up references to Jesus, where possible.

1. **Jesus' Birth:** (S3:35-51; 19:22-34; 21:91) - Mat 1:18-25, 2:1-23; Lk 1:26-80

2. **Jesus' Miracles:** (S3:49, 5:113-118) - Mat 14:13-21,15;32-38, 26:17-29

3. **Jesus' Teaching:** (S3:50-53, 5:119-121, 19:30-33) - Mat 5:1- 7:28

4. **Jesus' Death & Ascension:** S(2:87;3:55; 4:157-159; 5:19,120; 19:33) - Mat 26-27; Jn 12:31-34; Acts 2:22-24; 1 Cors 15:20-28

5. **Jesus' Titles & Descriptions:**

It can be helpful to work through this list with a Muslim friend and discuss the implications of the superlative titles and references given to Jesus in the Koran.

- He is Creator of Life (S3:49: 5:113) n.b. he was existing before life began - Jn 1:4

- He is the Messiah, i.e. promised by all the prophets and a prophet promised from among the Jews (S3:45; 4:171; 5:19; 9:30) - Deut 18:18

- He is a sign from God (S3:50; 19:21; 23:50; 46:61) - Mat 24:30-31; 25:31-46

- He came for Israel (S3:49) and all nations (S 21:91) - Jn 1:9,10,29; 3:16-17; 4:42

- His coming has significance in this world & for eternity (S 3:45; 43:61)

- He is blessed (S19:31) - Mat 21:9; Lk 13:35

- He is a mercy from God (S19:21) - Lk 1:76-78

- The Spirit of God was on him (S2:253) - Mat 3:16-17

The Theological Barrier

7

- He is the Word of Truth (S19:34) - Jn 1:17, 14:6

- He is an example (S43:57-59) - Jn 13:15

- He is illustrious and held in honour (S3:45) - Mat 25:31, 32; Jn 17:5,24

- He is the Word of God (S3:39, 45; 4:171)…n.b. a 'word' is equal to a 'thought' or the 'mind' and soul itself; it is the closest thing to the speaker - Gen 1: 3,6,9,11,14,20,24,26,29; Is 43:12; Heb 1:1-3

- He is one of the "nearest to God" (S3:45) - Jn 14:6; 20:17; Acts 7:55, 56

- He is the Spirit of God (S2:87, 253; 4:171; 5:113; 15:29; 21:91) - Mat 12:15-28; Acts 10:38

- He was an apostle or messenger of God (S2:253; 10:47) - Jn 6:29, 9:4, 12:44-50

The meaning of 'Son of God'

- Jesus was born of a virgin (S19:16-35). God did this by the Holy Spirit (S21: 91).

- The father 'role' is taken by God who initiated the conception (S19:21-22).

- The Bible term "begotten" (Jn 3:16) is not helpful to a Muslim as it can give the impression that God physically fathered Jesus like a human being. The Greek says "mono-genesis", which means God's 'only born'. God sent Christ 'The Word of God' via the natural birth process of conception, gestation and delivery in order that *"The Word"* should *"become flesh and live for a while among us"* (Jn 1:14). See also Mat1:18-23; Lk1:26-35.

- Jesus came out from the corporate unity of the Godhead. He came from God who is the 'source' (Arabic *"assnad"*) or origin.

- Jesus existed before He came to earth (S3:49, 5:113) - Jn1:1-14; Heb 1:1-13 n.b. Jesus became the Son of God when he was born on earth.

- The "I Am" statements indicate his divinity while the title 'Son of God' emphasises his humanity.

The Crucifixion of Jesus

Although the Koran appears to deny the crucifixion (S4:157-158) it also admits to Jesus' death and raising up to God (S3:55; 19:33-34). Who is to say when this took place? Muslims say it will happen at the end of the world, but on what authority? Historic evidence for the Crucifixion is found in the secular writings of Pliny, Tacitus and Josephus who were alive at the time.

The Communication Barrier

'Christians and Muslims use different words to refer to the same thing and the same word to refer to different things.'

The fourth barrier to successful befriending between Muslims and Christians is communication. This process seems doomed from the start because we tend to speak past one another.

We have seen that both verbal and non-verbal communication are as important as each other. This means that how we dress, how we speak, our attitude and our behaviour say more about us than our words. When we have grasped this point, we are ready to turn to the potential problems with our words.

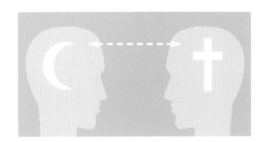

The Process of Communication:

Communication is basically about three things…

1. transmitting a message

2. how that message is understood

3. checking that it has been received in the way we intended

If all three are achieved then successful communication has taken place. If the hearer understands something different from the meaning intended, there has been a failure i.e. the wrong thing has been communicated.

It can be discouraging to find out that many Christian terms and expressions have quite different meaning for a Muslim. Here are some examples of the communication barrier in action. The following list is intended to show how a Muslim friend could understand some Christian words.

Word	Muslim understanding	Acknowledgement - Aubrey Whitehouse *'Watch Your Language'*
God	distant, capricious, unpredictable, unknowable	
Jesus Christ	prophet of Islam, never died, translated to heaven, will return to marry have children & bring Islam to the world	
Holy Spirit	the Angel Gabriel	
Trinity	a polytheistic idol. Some Muslims think it is God the father, Mary the mother & Jesus their son	
Bible	originally containing the word of God, now changed, and corrupted	
sin	a mistake categorised in a hierarchy by God. 'God leads astray the evil doers and God does what He will' (S 4:52). Sin is to be improved upon next time, not inborn, not inevitable, there is no 'original sin'	

The Communication Barrier

Word	Muslim understanding
faith	a mental assent to the articles of belief - 'No soul can believe except by the will of God' (S10:99)
repentance	this is determined by God's initiative and control. 'God guides to Him all who are penitent (S13:27-30), 'No choice have they (men) (S28:67). Muslims might see their response to God's enabling as a stiffened resolve based on feeling sorry for getting caught
forgiveness	God decides to offer clemency, only known for certain on Judgement Day 'He punishes whom He pleases and has mercy on whom He pleases' (S29:20)
guilt	the shame of being caught
redemption	the paying of compensation for a sin. Only seven mentions in the Koran. This only place where sacrifice occurs is Abraham sacrificing his son in S37:99-110 where the Koran claims that it is Ishmael (not Isaac) who is ransomed rather than Abraham n.b. This is not linked to sin.
salvation	uncertain, obtained by belief and good works, God delivering you out of trouble like King David the psalmist
sanctification	outward performance and appearance, obedience to ceremonial ritual
love	tendency to think of the erotic in humans, conditional in God, "love" is not one of the 99 Names of God
heaven	male domain of sensuous and erotic pleasure
hell	place of torment for those who find God's disapproval on Judgement Day
New birth	unheard of
grace	not understood, synonymous with mercy, God deciding to be kind
demons	the *jinn*, neutral spirit entities capable of good or evil, need appeasing sometimes by magical ocultic practices

Photo courtesy of Frontiers International ©

Ideas for getting alongside to communicate with a Muslim friend:

a. pray asking God to develop His love for him/her in you

b. introduce yourself and learn to greet in their language

c. send halal sweets and a card on feast days

d. visit your friend in his/her home

e. offer to pray when there are problems

f. develop a natural, agenda-free relationship

g. offer practical help e.g. baby-sit their children, English learning

h. be sensitive to possible points of 'felt-need' e.g. illness, infertility

i. become known to the senior male in the household

j. have spiritual chats or read the Bible one-to-one

k. hold international friendship evenings in your church or home

l. offer a multi-cultural kindergarten in your church

Neighbours in a Plural Society

'…pluralism means everyone affirms his values and we all live in tolerance. But in private schools Jews don't meet Christians. Christians don't meet Hindus. Everybody meets nothing. There is so much intermarrying because it is non-Jewish Jews who marry non-Christian Christians. Jews for nothing marry Christians for nothing. They get on because they affirm nothing. They have everything in common - nothing.'

Dennis Prager (Jewish author)

There is a tension in British society. On the one hand Britain is an island nation, which in the past has tended to instil a caution about perceived 'outsiders'. At the same time 'outsiders' have been arriving on the island for centuries. Since the 1950s, Britain has become a thoroughly 'pluralist' society.

With the addition of the more recent European influence, the notion of 'political correctness' has gained icon status and reigns almost unchallenged. Someone has said 'anything less than total toleration will no longer be tolerated'. Equal rights are now given to everyone. No one can be discriminated against on the basis of age, gender, race, religion or sexual orientation - a mantra of the EU.

We do not mind making people feel badly about smoking, drugs or racism but Christians (and Muslims) are under pressure not to be judgemental about chaotic sexual ethics and a morality of convenience. In such a confused society the notion of the 'uniqueness of Jesus Christ' is being challenged. The very idea of having the "right" to share good news with someone from another faith community is now seriously questioned - even within evangelical churches. As a result, the question "Who is My Neighbour?" becomes even more critical. Can you recognise a neighbour when you see one? Clearly it is not so much our "right" as our "responsibility" to share the Good News about Jesus.

Neighbours in a Plural Society

9

Immigration to Britain - see how they come

700 B.C.	Celtic peoples arrived
43 A.D.	Romans arrived to occupy including soldiers from Gaul, Spain, Germany, Balkans, Asia Minor and even Africa
400 A.D.	Saxons, Angles & Jutes from Europe began raiding the island
800 A.D.	Viking raids started from Scandinavia
1066 A.D.	invasion by William the Conqueror of Normandy
12th Century	Irish economic immigration to England
16th Century	Swarthy southern Europeans were thought to be spies for the Pope, the Jesuits or the King of Spain. Black Africans arrived in slavery
17th Century	Oliver Cromwell welcomed Jews back after expulsion by Edward 1,300 years earlier. They made London a financial capital of the world
Late 17th Century	Half a million Protestant French Huguenots brought weaving and silk working to Britain, fleeing persecution by King Louis XIV
18th Century	Thousands of Scots moved to England to seek their fortune after the Act of Union. Jewish immigration continued.
18th Century	Catholic French aristocrats (previously the persecutors of the Huguenots) fled to Britain to escape the French Revolution
Early 19th Century	A monkey survived the shipwreck of a French vessel. It was thought to be a Frenchmen and hung. Chinese seamen began arriving.
Late 19th Century	Arrivals from America and British colonies
Early 20th Century	Arrival of Jews while Eastern and southern Europeans received sanctuary in Britain during World War II and afterwards
Mid 20th Century	Arrival of economic migrants from the Caribbean and Asia helped build the British economy
Late 20th Century	Arrival of migrants from the Muslim World, Africa and South East Asians have come on professional assignments, to spend money on medical treatment, as students, or as political asylum-seekers and refugees

From Patrick Sookdheo (Ed) 1991

In Luke 10:25-37 Jesus met a young man who was successful and upwardly mobile with mixed motives and a hidden agenda to justify his individualistic and racist philosophy, which he expected Jesus to affirm. The young man asks *"What shall I do to inherit eternal life?"* (v25). Jesus answers a question with a question *"What is written in the Law? How do you understand it?"* (v26). Like many of us, the young

Acknowledgement to
Colin Chapman - 'You go and do the same'

Neighbours in a Plural Society

man gives the pat answer "*Love the LORD your God with all your heart, soul, strength and mind* (from Deut 6.5) *and love your neighbour as yourself*" (from Lev 19:18). (v27). "*Correct*", says Jesus "*Do this and live*" (v28). He didn't co-operate with the agenda behind the question so the young man is forced to reveal more.

He asks "*And who is my neighbour?*" (v29). For him a 'neighbour' is someone of the same race, social class, income bracket and even theological position i.e. "people like me". This is a form of idolatry where we do not have a god, but a neighbour, in our own image and likeness! The parable, which follows, is a shocking reversal of the accepted social norm. It highlights God's heart for all races. In short, Jesus is teaching the Old Testament principle '*The immigrant living amongst you in your land must be treated as one of your native born. Love him as yourself*'. (Lev 19:33)

In the parable, an anonymous man is mugged. Like Western Muslims today, Samaritans were a politely tolerated immigrant minority with the legal right of residence. Samaritans, practised a corrupt form of Judaism. In the same way some Christians see Islam as a corrupt form of Christianity. The first two people to pass by the anonymous mugged man fail to recognise the man in need as the 'neighbour' in question.

- the Priest and Levite were full of religious superiority (v31-32)

- the Samaritan challenges Jewish racial and cultural superiority (v33)

Jesus then moves in for the kill - "*Which was the neighbour to the man in need? (v36). "He who showed mercy*" says the young man. Jesus concludes "*You go and do the same*" (v37).

How can we do the same? Who is the 'neighbour' for me in the real world? I cannot help everyone. How do I choose? What does God want me to do? As individuals we can best respond to those around us everyday, but as a local church we can respond to need in four 'neighbourhood' fields …

- Jerusalem (locally)...................................... mono-culturally

- Judea (regionally & nationally)..................... mono & bi-culturally

- Samaria (adjacent nations continentally)....... bi-culturally

- to the ends of the earth (globally)................. cross-culturally

'The very view of reality that gives rise to the beliefs and practices of ordinary Muslims is in many respects closer to the biblical one than to the missionary's own mechanistic, scientific world view'.

Dr. Bill Musk

"*The love of Christ constrains us…*" (2 Cors 5:14) i.e. Hems us in like the banks of a great river flowing out of the heart of God. God leads us out of our Jerusalem into the world of need among all races, cultures and faiths i.e. the poor, the widows, the fatherless, the oppressed, the needy, the disenfranchised and the sexually confused.

As Christians, we are not an end in ourselves, we are God's means to *His* greater end – the blessing of the not-yet-churched! A New Testament understanding of mission is that we exist for our neighbours in the 'regions beyond'. I am encouraged by Worcester Assemblies of God Church where there is a sign

Neighbours in a Plural Society

9

Photo courtesy of Interserve ©

over the exit of the building saying - 'The ends of the earth start here!'. This is a clear statement of a New Testament understanding of the missionary nature of the local church.

Natural ways to meet Muslims

Natural friendship is the goal of our interaction with Muslims. Here are some ideas about where we are likely to see this happen.

- By using their business services

- In the work place

- Making a point of greeting them in the street (Mat 5:47)

- Joint community service projects

- Door-to-door
  Though less natural, door-to-door is proving a useful way of first contact when accompanied by the Jesus Video or a questionnaire. Through this we can personally put a Gospel or extracts of scripture material into the hands of Muslims in their own language. This can be especially welcomed at feast days.

- Telling your own story
  When speaking with people from Muslim cultures it always helps if you can use simple expressions and picture language. Speak less of personal relationship with God and more about acceptance by Him and His answers to prayer and activity in your experience. Do speak about the joy of personal prayer where you say what you want, not what you are required to, and God answers. Use the Scripture wherever you can. Remember you are a "Believer in Jesus" and always speak about Him clearly and simply. Do not talk about your church, denomination or Christianity in general.

Visiting a Muslim home

i. Men visit men and women visit women. Men only visit when it is likely that the man will be at home. If he is not, a man will not be admitted unless a woman is with him. Children are often on door duty and can relay messages without the caller even seeing an adult. A good time to visit women is early afternoon.

ii. Good visiting times include the afternoon of the first day of a feast (*Eid*), births, circumcisions, deaths, engagements, weddings, completion of the Hajj pilgrimage or even on promotion at work.

iii. Leaving the gathering early on a public occasion can be misunderstood so try not to be the first to go.

iv. At the time of celebration it is good to take halal sugared almonds or sweets.

v. Some Muslim households will take their shoes off to enter the living room and sometimes slippers are provided for guests.

Acknowledgement to Francis Iliff 'Salam Alekum' - Understanding Muslim Culture.

Neighbours in a Plural Society

9

vi. Refreshments such as tea, coffee, juice or fruit is served to a guest soon after arrival. This is an extended way to prolong the greetings phase of the visit. Don't hurry this because it is a statement of welcome, a bonding mechanism. Several visits may be made before an important topic is broached as in the book of Esther (see Esther 5:4; 7:1).

vii. Ask indirectly after "the family" not someone's spouse or female members of the family.

viii. During group conversation in a conservative Muslim home, do not be surprised if each gender addresses their remarks to someone of the same gender, even though they may be intended for someone of the opposite gender in the room. This is normal.

ix. Be careful about complimenting an object as it can indicate your desire to have it. To compliment a child may be thought to invoke the 'evil eye' of the devil to inflict harm.

x. Muslims may ask a lot of personal questions such as - How old are you? Are you married if not, why not? How many children do you have? How much do you earn? How much did you pay for your house? Try to take this in your stride. It is a way of assessing where to place you in their social system of relationships.

xi. When ending a visit it is important to farewell everyone in the room starting with the oldest and most honoured person then working downwards. As a guest you may be escorted to the front door, to your car or even to the bus stop or tube station. This is a cultural honour (see Genesis 18:16).

Meals

i. Obviously this is a more advanced form of relationship. As in the Bible, meals are an excellent way to develop relationships, though normally conversation happens before and after rather than around the table.

ii. See *halal* food in Appendix 4.

iii. Guests are served first, then the senior males in order and then children. The females of the family may eat in a separate room.

iv. If you leave food on the plate it is not a sign the food is not liked, it means the food is actually good and the host has succeeded in filling you up.

v. A Muslim who is not hungry may take some of everything on offer and only taste each. This is because showing courtesy for hospitality is more important than eating a lot. Pressing a guest three times to have a second helping is often cultural. It is used as a signal that the host means it and that the guest's refusal indicates they are not greedy.

'Muslims need to see Christ in the ordinary Christian. It is unfortunate that many of us do not live in such a manner as to influence the minds of Muslims'.

Rt Rev Riah Abul Assal
(Bishop in Jerusalem)

Neighbours in a Plural Society

9

Greetings cards

Send greeting cards in vernacular languages (available from CPO, see Appendix 3). It is also acceptable to give halal sugared almonds or sweets.

Videos

Story telling is part of many Muslim cultures so videos are an effective and attractive medium to them. There is good material available in English and vernacular languages (see Appendix 3). The *Jesus* film is one of the most widely used, though this is best placed with Muslims who are already showing interest in the gospel. A follow-up questionnaire and Bible study is available in English for the *Jesus Film*.

Special local church events

It is better to use dates, which can include the family e.g. Christmas, Father's Day or Mother's Day. Where possible it is better to include national music and/or simple songs or psalms in vernacular languages, drama and dance with a short message, which emphasises story telling. Plenty of time is needed afterwards for eating. Appropriate Christian literature can be available in vernacular languages. Welcomers should be men dealing with men and women with women.

Photo courtesy of AWM International ©

Discussing the Good News with a Muslim Friend

"Muslims need to be met within the context of Islam. The spiritual revolution must occur from within his own socio-cultural context. We must carry the living Christ with all his power to heal, exorcise and save into the real world of ordinary Muslims, and trust him to meet heart hunger without implicit condemnation of their cultural heritage. Can Christ trust us that much?"

Rev Dr. Bill Musk

The key question is how can I talk to a Muslim friend about the Good News. The first thing to remember is that until you can use the expression "friend" of a particular Muslim you are not in the best position to discuss the Good News with them. It is easier to work at befriending first. Friendship is the 'first base'. This may take some time but there is no rush.

This approach is not 'pie in the sky' because, even from within Islam itself, Muslims are encouraged to relate to non-Muslims with respect (S16:125) and in the *'best possible way'* (S29:46), even to *'make friends of enemies'* (S41:34). Remember, friendship is time-consuming. There is no quick fix in this business (see 2 Corinthians 4:1-2), which is partly why Christians are easily tempted to ignore the issue all together.

When we are gaining the trust of a Muslim friend, we can start the process of discussing spiritual issues. The more trust between us, the more right we have to speak. Here are some ideas on how to do this.

- Use your personal story (see 1 Thess 2:8)

- Be content to explain the Good News one aspect at a time (Mat 13:3)

- Use picture language where possible.

- Use illustrations - articles or books can often get an idea over better than discussion

- Encourage your friend to read the Gospels for themselves, preferably not Mark as this begins *"This is the gospel of Jesus Christ the Son of God"*.

Discussing the Good News with a Muslim Friend

- Try to help your friend understand the reasons why the gospel is needed i.e. our inability to help ourselves and that we are in need of the 'lift of grace'.

- In a word - try to address heart-hunger not mental prejudice.

- Ask for the space to explain the gospel fully uninterrupted before discussing questions.

Some basic Muslim phrases:

Arabic:

marhaba! - hello
(informal non-religious)

asslaamu alaikum - peace on you
(formally used for hello and goodbye, like shalom alekhem in Hebrew)

wi alaikum assalaam - and peace on you too *(response to the above)*

al hamdu lillah - Praise God
(expression of thankfulness)

ma assalaama - goodbye

eid al-mubarak - Happy feast day

Ramadan ikareem - Happy Ramadan

Urdu & Persian:

Suber khair - good morning

> *"Dialogue is the serious address and response between two persons, in which the being and truth of each is confronted by the being and truth of the other. It involves relationship and words and seeks to know life through the other person".*
> *Reuel Howe*

Proclamatory Dialogue

An important approach to develop is to try to put yourself into the shoes of a Muslim. It is possible to ask things, which rather than challenging them, can affirm them as an individual seeker after God and help them feel comfortable to answer more honestly. For example "How does it feel to fast and what spiritual benefit do you feel?". As trust grows we earn the right to go deeper. This is the essence of 'Proclamatory Dialogue', which is a helpful tool. Proclamatory Dialogue is simply dialogue in which we have something to proclaim (see Appendix 2). To enter into this with a Muslim friend we need to take the initiative.

One of the first steps is to have a go at using social greetings in the vernacular language of your friend (see side column).

Here are some ideas for conversation openers.

9/11 - How does your friend feel about the events of 11 September 2001 and their aftermath?

CULTURE & LANGUAGE - What about his/her family place of origin, their customs and language? (i.e. related to birth, weaning of infants, coming of age, courtship, marriage, death).

FEAST DAYS - What is the significance for them of a recent or forthcoming feast?

PRAYER - What does it mean to their relationship "to" God? Explain the contrast of Christian offer of a relationship "with" God through Jesus Christ?

Does your friend pray prayers of *du'a* (personal petition in their own words) in addition to *salat* (prescribed) prayer? If God is almighty and everything comes as 'fate' from his decrees, what is the purpose of prayer at all?

THE ISLAMIC CREED - "There is no god but God and Muhamad is the Messenger of God". What does it mean to them? Compare with the Lord's Prayer (Lk 11:2-4).

Discussing the Good News with a Muslim Friend

FASTING - Ask about the Feast of Ramadan. What is their personal experience of it and what spiritual benefits come from it for them personally? (Isaiah 58).

AMULETS - These are charms to ward off evil. They are for protection from dark powers. Do they think God prefers his word to be around our necks or in our hearts - why? (Ps 119:11)

THE VEIL - The why, when and how of wearing the veil (*higab* or *burqa*). Ask why they think Christian women do not wear a veil? (Is 61:10; 1 Pet 3:1-6)

HALAL FOODS - What does your friend think about its significance? Where do they buy these food stuffs from?

ALMSGIVING - Compare Muslim and Christian ways of giving. (2 Cors 9:6-15)

PILGRIMAGE - What is the significance of pilgrimage in Islam? Have they been to Mecca and what meaning did it have for them? (Jn 14:1-6)

FORGIVENESS - What does this mean in Islam? Does your Muslim have to wait for Judgement Day? Has your friend ever asked for it and received it - did they know they had been forgiven?

FEAR - What does your friend fear most - death, hell, sickness, demon possession, loss of face?

CRISIS - What does your Muslim friend do in a crisis - go to a friend, family, an Imam, magical practitioner - other? (Ps 121)

SALVATION HISTORY - Trace some key Koranic figures (e.g. Adam, Abraham, Moses & Jesus). What about their significance for Muslims and Christians?

SCRIPTURE - What does your friend think about the Bible and the Koran? (Gen 22; Ex 12; Num 19:9; Jn 3:14; Rom 6:23; Eph 2:8; 1 Tim 2:4-5; Heb 9:22; 10:1-8,12)

THE NEWS - What does your friend think and how do they feel about Al-Qaeda? Osama Bin-Laden? George W Bush Jr? Saddam Hussein?

'The gift of the gospel must come wrapped in you!'

Photo Steve Ecll ©

Discussing the Good News with a Muslim Friend

We can find the principle of proclamatory dialogue in the life of Jesus. Even as a boy, he models this. Notice how he genuinely listened while humbly having something to say. Observe him doing five things in his discourse with the elders in the Temple in Luke 2:45-46.

i.   sitting among them

ii. listening

iii. asking questions

iv. gaining and exhibiting understanding

v.   giving answers to questions asked of him

This is the pattern for us to follow with our Muslim friends. Remember that you are only a link in the chain of God's dealings with them. They may even be further on than you think. For example Cornelius' story just prior to meeting the Apostle Peter in Acts10:1-6. God was aware of Cornelius' prayers even before he heard the Good News from Peter and believed. This tells us something about God's dealings with Muslims even before they believe in Jesus? For some Muslim believers in Jesus it is a process of God's activity in their lives rather than a crisis of intervention that brings them to faith in Christ.

God is often dealing with Muslims and answering their prayers before they begin to follow Jesus.

Handling Controversy

It is easy to get into controversy with a Muslim so do not start arguments if at all possible. Controversial issues include - the Bible being changed, Christians worshipping three gods, Jesus being the biological offspring of a sexual union between God and Mary, Jesus dying on the Cross, the West being both immoral and Christian by definition, Christians supporting the political State of Israel, Christians drinking alcohol and eating pork, the person of Mohamad.

- Resist the temptation to quarrel (2 Tim 2:23-26). Try to avoid blatantly criticising Islam (Mat 7:1-5).

- Work at removing misunderstanding by asking why your Muslim friend thinks as he or she does.

- Always try to distinguish between what are essential and non-essential, central and peripheral, primary and secondary issues within Christian and Islamic belief. This helps us not to become deviated into unhelpful cul-de-sacs.

- Be prepared to admit and even ask forgiveness for any violations committed against Muslims by Christians in the past and present (Ps 106:6; Roms 2:24).

- Take every opportunity to say what you believe and why you believe it (1 Pet 3:15).

- The aim is not to win an argument but the person. It is possible to lose the argument and still win the person if love is our attitude.

- Be patient. Muslim people take time to assimilate and respond to new truth, just as we do.

How some Muslims are Finding Christ

'Perhaps it is time to stop expecting the Muslim to see the love of God in the cross of Christ. It might be easier for him to glimpse there something of Christ's loyalty to his Father, something of the Father's glory in watching his Son obey him to the end, vindicating family honour.'

Rev Dr. Bill Musk

Muslims are finding their way to faith in Jesus Christ in various parts of the world. In certain countries there have been 'people movements' where whole families, clans, villages or people groups believe the Good News at the same time. However, this is much more rare and most often, they come in a steady trickle as individuals.

God is clearly at work in new ways amongst Muslims and we should be encouraged by this. Again we must stress that they are not becoming "Christians". This is a politically loaded and even dangerous term. Rather they are becoming "followers of Jesus". But how is this happening? In my experience there are four ways (or a mixture of the four), in which Muslims most frequently turn to Christ. These are as follows…

- Reading the Bible with an open mind
- Knowing a Christian over a period of time
- Sincere comparison and search through the Koran to the Bible
- Supernatural intervention of God

A survey, which bears this out has been recently conducted by an American theological institution. In the survey 600 believers in Jesus from a Muslim background were questioned. The subjects spoke of the reasons why they left the religious component of Muslim culture to follow Jesus in spite of persecution, hardship and death threats. The study found that…

a. a growing number of Muslims are turning to Christ all over the world

b. 'house group' churches are mushrooming all over the Middle East as these believers are drawn to fellowship with others of similar experience

c. the most often cited reasons for conversion include…

   i. The certainty of salvation in Christ compared to the uncertainty of the Islamic tradition, which says that the bridge to heaven is only as wide as a human

A Story:

'Farida is from a Muslim family. She became a Christian in the summer of 2001 during an outreach at the chapel of a Christian hospital where she had received loving treatment by medical staff.

There was concern about Farida's nurture in Christ because she is illiterate. She was urged to listen to Christian radio. One evening she found her elder brother listening to the same broadcast and discovered that he too had become a Christian while working on a farm where he had made friends with a Christian. Farida's brother is educated and reads the Scripture to her, which encourages her.'

How some Muslims are Finding Christ

hair. Not even good deeds can guarantee a safe crossing. According to Muslims even the prophet Muhammed does not know if he will make it to heaven.

ii. The character of Christ being attractive - his humility, non-retaliation and love for the weak and marginalised.

iii. The character of Christians - their concern for justice and works of mercy to the needy, including Muslims, their tranquility and inner peace.

iv. Over 25% have had supernatural intervention by dreams, visions of angels and/or Jesus, healings and miraculous occurrences. Jesus has even spoken to them and announced the healing of a loved-one, which then happens.

Testimonies:

An Egyptian man was reading Luke's Gospel and reached chapter 3 when a strong wind entered the room and a voice said "I am Jesus Christ, whom you hate. I am the Lord you are seeking". The man said "I cried and cried and decided to follow Jesus that day".

An Afghan man was imprisoned by the Taliban. Having nothing to do in jail he started reading a dictionary and his eyes fell on the word "Jesus". Every time he read it a supernatural presence filled the cell. This triggered his search for the meaning of the word and his conversion. He is now a fearless evangelist within Afghanistan.   (Source Friday Fax 2001)

A Story:

"For as long as I can remember I felt attracted to Islam. I memorised the Qur'an at the age of six - even before I'd gone to primary school. I was certain that Islam was the religion of truth and Christianity the religion of blasphemy. I avoided the Bible - I thought it was a distorted book.

"The first time I set eyes on a Bible was when I was at college. At that time, I spent every spare minute studying the Bible and the Qur'an side-by-side, determined to prove the distortion of the Bible. I was confident that I would succeed.

"It wasn't long before doubts started to fill my mind. During one of my study sessions I came across John 3:16. That night I had a dream in which I heard a beautiful voice repeating the verse over and over. The dream came back, a second time and then a third time. The following morning, I went to see the friend who'd given me the Bible. He told me that God was speaking to me, but I wasn't convinced. So I challenged him, 'If I hear this voice again today, I'll be a Christian with you. If I don't then you'll have to be a Muslim with me'. He agreed and I went home.

"That night I heard the voice again speaking to me three times. All I could do was to accept Jesus Christ as Lord and Saviour of my life. Following my conversion, I was expelled by my family and thrown out of college. But with the help of the Open Doors organisation I was able to go and study at a Bible school abroad."   (Source: Open Doors)

Mentoring Believers from Islam

Photo courtesy of AWM International ©

'Converts' or 'Proselytes'?

We need to be clear what we mean by "conversion" from Islam. This can mean …

a. individual repentance and trust in Christ (Acts 20:21) i.e. a change of heart-allegiance from the religious aspect of Muslim culture to Christ. Less helpfully, it has also come to mean…

b. individual withdrawal of the new believer from their Muslim community and cultural roots.

We need to affirm the first meaning and shun the second. When a new believer in Jesus from Islam withdraws from his or her culture it is self-defeating because it can actually attract ostracism. Sadly, in the past, new believers from Islam have actually been encouraged to leave their culture. For example by changing their Muslim name to a, so-called, "Christian" name. In this way "Ahmad" became "Peter". Some people call this "extraction evangelism".

This sort of Westernising of new believers from Islam could even make opposition from their community worse; and rightly so, we might say. Like a Jewish person, if a Muslim comes to faith in Christ, he or she does not stop being ethnically or culturally Muslim. So care needs to be taken with believers from Muslim backgrounds that their conversion remains primarily of the heart i.e. *to* Jesus Christ and *from* Islam. It is not conversion away from Muslim culture per se. The Gospel only ever redeems us from the negative aspects of any culture. We would not expect a Westerner to withdraw from their community after conversion. Indeed we are most effective witnesses at this early stage of our new Christian experience. It is ironic that we place these expectations on our Muslim friends when their background is often closer to the biblical norm than our Western culture.

Rather than asking believers from Islam to withdraw entirely from their community, we need to encourage them to ask God to show them what to do. It is always

Mentoring Believers from Islam

12

easier when the Holy Spirit teaches them which aspects of Muslim culture need 'redeeming' and which aspects the Bible affirms. Ultimately it is only God who can show them how to be a loyal follower of Jesus in their own community and culture.

When the new believer from Islam is coerced into adopting aspects of Western culture in order to be a follower of Christ, they are in reality a "proselyte". This sort of cultural transfer used to happen when Gentile proselytes were expected to adopt Jewish culture in addition to their believing in the God of the Jews.

The early Apostles, however, did not choose this pattern, rather they aimed for "conversion". Paul in particular became angry over this very issue when he found it going on in the Galatian church. In the New Testament, non-Jewish believers were free to choose to attach themselves to the church in their own way. Gentile proselytes to Judaism did so while being unable to become ethnically or culturally Jewish. In the same way Gentile "converts" joined the mainly Jewish church while keeping their Greek name, identity, culture and relational network (see Mk 5:1-20). As a result the Good News spread due, in part, to the Apostles' conclusion on the matter as follows…

"It seemed good to us and to the Holy Spirit not to lay a greater burden on you other than that you abstain from eating food offered to idols, eating the blood of strangled animals and sexual immorality" (Acts 15:28).

Mentoring believers from Muslim backgrounds

Conversion:
Conversion, for a Muslim, like anyone else is usually a mixture of 'crisis' and 'process'. Sometimes there are several crises along the way. The 'process' can be seen in the rational search of a Nicodemus while the 'crisis' is the radical Damascus Road of a Paul. Both are valid. Therefore the discipling of believers from Muslim backgrounds usually starts *before* their heart-allegiance moves from Islam to Jesus Christ.

Persecution:
Persecution is not inevitable when Muslims follow Christ especially if they are from an open-minded or educated family. However, in conservative and less educated households it is more likely.

'The close-knit Muslim community is an entrenched cultural web enmeshing people in deep loyalty to the system. The underlying adherence to customs, community and family make individual decisions for Christ well nigh impossible without fatally injuring those relationships' (Patrick Johnstone)

Mentoring Believers from Islam

Muslims who change their allegiance to Jesus Christ will therefore likely face some form of reaction. The opposition will be on a spectrum from harmless antagonism, to actual ejection from the home, to outright persecution or even death. This will likely come from their extended family and community. We need to think this reality through but not be deterred by it. It is an attempt to protect the individual from error and the family from shame.

The underlying basis for this opposition is the Koran's statement that anyone leaving Islam is committing 'apostasy' and is therefore a blasphemer (S2:217; 3:90; 4:89;16:106-107). As such they are worthy of death by any relative of the family upon which the shame has been brought. Each new believer's experience is different depending on their circumstances.

- It is ideal when the whole family or community converts, but this is rarely the case.

- There is also the need to think in terms of mission to the whole 'household'.

- Prominent families understandably tend to be more reactionary about the humiliation of family members leaving Islam.

Photo courtesy of Frontiers International ©

'Ikrma Ali burned some people and the news reached Ibn Abbas who said "Had I been in his place I would not have burned them. As the Prophet said "Don't punish anybody with Allah's punishment". Though no doubt I would have killed them, for the Prophet said "If somebody (i.e. a Muslim) discards his religion, kill him".'

(Hadith Vol 4:52, 'Fighting for Allah's Cause' Ch 149 No.260 (pg 160-161)

It is good to know the Bible is no stranger to suffering and persecution. Here are some references, which may help - Mat 10:24-25; Acts 5:40-42; 1 Pet 4:12-16; Heb 13:10-14. The tragic stories of persecution of believers from Muslim background, when it does happen, suggests to us that more local churches need to identify 'safe-houses' where endangered believers from Muslim backgrounds can be placed for their safety.

A Story:

'...But when my family found out about my conversion they felt disgraced. They realised that putting me in an asylum would only bring more shame, so they asked an experienced Muslim Sheikh to talk to me. I prayed silently "Lord may your Son be glorified! I'm in trouble now; please deliver me!" At the end of our time the Sheikh turned to my father and said "Sir, your son is alright. It is you who needs healing".

After several incidents like this my father beat me, but I felt no pain. My family cut me off, refusing to have meals with me. Even my clothes were washed and rinsed in a separate container.

Mentoring Believers from Islam

After seeing me come out of church one day, my father was so angry he ended up by tearing my clothes and throwing me out of the house. Since then I have been moving from place to place knowing that my new family is the family of God"…'.

A Muslim young man from the south of Egypt

Secret believing went on in the Bible:

Old Testament examples include Esther (Esther 2:8-11; 4:12-14; 7:3,4), Elijah (1 Kgs 17:1-6; 19:1-9), Naaman (2 Kgs 5:17-19).

New Testament examples include Nicademus (John 3:1-10. 50-52), the general public (John 7.12-13, 12:42-43) and Joseph of Arimathea (John 19:38-42).

Confession remains vital - Mat 10:32-33; Rom 10:9-10. We have to decide where the balance is.

'Secret Believing':

If or when opposition does occur, it can be safer to take fellowship to the Muslim believer and not expect them to come to fellowship. Secret believers may feel the need to conceal their faith totally, or in certain situations, for a period of time. They may be in physical danger of reprisals or else they are not ready (or willing) to lose their position in the family pecking order i.e. perhaps as recipient to a legacy or assured employment in an extended family business.

There are differing opinions about what "confessing" Christ means (Rom 10:9,10). Paul did not specify who we confess to. It could be to God, to oneself or to a friend. It follows that different levels of secrecy are practised by Muslims who could be in mortal danger if they 'confessed' to the wrong person. Secret believers vary. For example they may only confess to God, sometimes only one other person knows, sometimes only a support group of reliable Christian friends know or even a member of their family might know. In some cases everyone but the family or Muslim community know because the believer has moved location in order to be a believer in Jesus openly.

Only God knows the best time to 'go public' in the family network as this can do more harm than good if it hardens the attitudes of others unnecessarily. The new believer needs to be supported as he or she prays through the issue of when that time might be. Ultimately it must be the decision of the new believer themselves as to when to make their allegiance to Jesus known.

Discipleship:

This sounds a cold metallic word but a 'disciple' is simply a *learner* or *student*. In reality discipleship is a relationship between a mentor and mentoree. Having said that, although it is normally a one-on-one activity, Jesus mentored groups of 3, 12 and 70.

The first letter of John says "*Our fellowship is with the Father and the Son… so you may have fellowship with us*". There is therefore a corporate aspect to discipleship. It can be healthy for a new believer from Islam to develop several Christian friends to learn from. The new believer is also likely to have Semitic spiritual insights, which may be enriching to their Western mentor.

Mentoring Believers from Islam

Discipleship involves teaching. We need to keep re-examining…

- exactly what Jesus instructs us to teach. (see Mat 28:18-20)
- what the early church understood by 'discipling' of newer believers (Acts 2:42; 18:11, 25-26; 19:9-10; Heb 6:1-2; 1 Pet 2:1-3, 4-5,9)
- the difference between biblical Christianity and Western culture.

Discipleship involves training. We will need to…

- Assess what Paul meant when he urged Timothy to 'rebuke, correct and train in righteousness'. (2 Tim 3.16).
- Decide whether a new believer from Islam should stop observing the Five Pillars n.b. Paul still observed certain Jewish rites for specific reasons. What do you think they might have been?

  a. Circumcision - Acts 16:1-3 (see also Acts 15:1-35; Gal 5:2-6)

  b. Nazarite Vow - Acts 18:18 (see also Num 6:18)

  c. Ritual purification - Acts 21:17-26

Enquirers:

Topics to include in discussion with enquirers include…

  a. The Oneness of God

  b. God has made man in His own image

  c. God has given His laws

  d. God judges man for disobeying His laws

  e. God told His prophets that He would come among them

  f. The Person & work of Jesus

  g. The disciples recognised Jesus as Messiah

  h. The Jews killed Jesus

  i. God raised Jesus from the dead

  j. God gives the Holy Spirit to believers in Jesus

(Acknowledgement - Vivienne Stacey - practical lessons for *Evangelism among Muslims*, 1988)

New Believers:

Topics to include in discussion with new believers include…

  a. salvation - repentance, faith, baptism in water & Spirit

  b. submission & obedience to Christ

  c. spiritual disciplines - prayer, bible study, worship, praise, fasting, giving, meditation

  d. breaking of bread

  e. fellowship

  f. healing

  g. relationship with God, other believers, other Muslims & family

---

Key aspects of popular Islamic misinformation to be removed:

1
You cannot know God

2
Jesus was just a man

3
Jesus did not die on the Cross

4
The Bible is unreliable

Mentoring Believers from Islam

Photo courtesy of AWM International ©

h. holiness of life

i. witness

j. the Trinity

k. family life & relationships

l. expressing the gospel into the Muslim mind-set

Mentoring through cultural issues include...

a. truth & honesty (Mat 5:37)

b. righteousness in finances (Amos 5:12)

c. legalism versus grace (Galatians)

d. marriage & family relationships

e. charms (Deut 17:10-11)

f. blessings, curses and vows - discernment about potential demonic activity in their situation

g. freedom from the unhelpful aspects of the past (Acts 19:18-20)

Fellowship:

- If it is inappropriate for the new believer to attend public church gatherings, home-based groups are safer and less provocative to other Muslims. The key issue here is that, wherever we are, we are the church - whether church gathered in worship or church scattered in the community. (see 1 Cors 12:27; 3:16-17; Heb 10:25)

- Local churches being used by God to nurture believers from Islam need to display the following characteristics …

a. open & caring communities

b. relating to the whole person outside the formal meeting setting

c. culturally flexible like the early church in Acts 6

d. ability to be a surrogate family or alternative '*Umma*' (community)

Water Baptism:

- Baptism in water is the cut-off point at which persecution may start. This is sometimes instigated by the powers of darkness expressing themselves through other Muslims who are open to such influence. Sometimes others are not even aware that the step of water baptism has taken place.

Worship:

Photo courtesy of Frontiers International ©

- One question we will face with new believers is whether or not we use alcoholic wine for Communion.

- To have Muslim background believers in Western churches may mean a need to encourage young women to dress more modestly, particularly in the summer months.

Mentoring Believers from Islam

Photo courtesy of Frontiers International ©

- For those from a traditional Muslim background it may offend them to see us put a Bible on the floor or prop church pianos up with it. These Muslims will be more comfortable seeing any holy book covered up and not with verses underlined. However, younger Westernised Muslims may actually be more impressed that a Bible is well used and written in.

- How might believers from Islam affect and/or be affected by our worship style for example our dancing, public hugging and shows of affection? These are issues to be thought through.

Authority:

- Some males may gravitate to male authority figures in the church and struggle with the idea of relating to 'ordinary' members of the flock.

- We need to wean the new believer away from the designated mentor and into the wider fellowship of believers.

- Sometimes spiritual deliverance is needed for males from 'controlling' spiritual influences which lead them to need to control.

Cross-Cultural relationships:

- Some Muslim males will need time to learn to relate naturally with females in a fellowship. They have a journey to make to unlearn their years of relating to women within Islam in an assumed dominant or superior way.

- In the present political climate in the West, the right to stay is a prized thing and can sometimes be achieved by a marriage certificate. When nurturing believers from Islam we need commonsense and a shrewd, realistic approach. While not resisting such liaisons out of some kind of unbending principle, we need to be ready to advise on the implications of any cross-cultural relationships, which may form.

- Both parties should go into this with eyes wide open and seriously think through the implications. There needs to be an openness to test God's will in the matter. It is advisable to bring in either an established believer from Muslim background and/or an experienced Christian with cross-cultural experience in an Islamic culture.

Appendix 1
Muslim equivalent to the Nicene Creed

THE NICENE CREED	A MUSLIM RESPONSE
We believe in one God, The Father the Almighty, Maker of heaven and earth, of all that is seen and unseen.	We must believe in one God Supreme and unknowable but for 99 Beautiful Names. He is maker of heaven and earth and all Worlds and beings - men, angels and jinn spirits.
We believe in one Lord Jesus Christ, The only Son of God, Eternally begotten of the Father, God from God, light from light, True God from true God, Begotten not made, Of one Being with the Father. By whom all things were made. For us men and for our salvation He came down from heaven; By the power of the Holy Spirit He became incarnate of the Virgin Mary, and was made man. For our sakes he was crucified under Pontius Pilate; He suffered death and was buried. On the third day he rose from the dead in accordance with the Scriptures. He ascended into heaven and is seated at the right hand of the Father. He will come again in glory to judge Both the living and the dead, and his kingdom will have no end.	We must believe in one Holy Qu'ran The miraculous and final message from God; A perfect conception eternally present with God. It descended supenaturally for our guidance. It proceeded from God by Whom all things were made. The Holy Qu'ran was delivered by dictation of the Angel Gabriel to the illiterate Prophet Muhamed (peace be upon him), who recited it to scribes, who wrote it down. The Holy Qu'ran is the final revelation of all the previous holy books i.e. Tawrat (Torah) of Moses, Zabur (Psalms) of David and Injil (Gospel) of]esus. These books emanate from the Eternal Tablet in heaven. The Prophet Isa (peace be upon him) was conceived supernaturally and born of the Virgin Maryam. He was sinless, unlike the other prophets. He did not die but another substituted for him while he was taken safely to heaven. The Prophet Isa (peace be upon him) will come again to marry, have a family, be a judge and a martyr for Islam.
We believe in the Holy Spirit, The Lord the Giver of Life, Who proceeds from me Father and the Son. With the Father and the Son He is worshipped and glorified. He has spoken through the Prophets.	We must believe in total submission to God based on fear (the highest religious sentiment), which is demonstrated by the performance of Pillars of duty. These are the source and way of Muslim life... 1. The Shahada (creed) 2. Prayer (x5 per day). 3. Fasting 4. Zakat (2.5% of disposable income) 5. Hajj (pilgrimage) 6. Jihad (struggle in the way of God)
We believe in one holy catholic and apostolic Church. We achnowledge one baptism for the forgiveness of sins. We look for the resurrection of the dead, and the Life of the world to come. AMEN	We must believe in one "Umma" or household of Islam. It is catholic in its duty of belief and practice, which are one; It is apostolic in its mission to the world until the Judgement Day when all men (Mohamad included) will be at the mercy of God and must await their fate.

Appendix 2
Useful Words and Explanations

A

Abrogation

This is a law of Koranic interpretation, which stresses the chronology of a verse (*aya*). Wherever there is apparent contradiction between verses, the later revelation is given prime of place over the earlier revelation (S2:106; 16:101; 22:52). A valid question to politely ask a Muslim friend is whether God changed his mind. The reason why there is the need to abrogate verses in the first place is neither asked nor answered in Muslim teaching.

C

Creation

Unlike the six days of creation in the Torah and Bible, different Suras of the Koran teach the creation of the world in a different numbers of days. In contrast to the Bible, the impression is given more clearly in the Koran that a 'day' does not necessarily mean 24 hours. Today, Muslims tend to support any science, which supports the Koranic view of the order, balance and purpose of the created world.

Communism & Islam

Islam has similarities with Communism. Both have the idea of the corporate society (Umma). Both are committed to the equality of all individuals in an egalitarian way. Both regulate society very firmly according to a set creed established by a charismatic founder. Both punish severely departure from the set doctrine. Political liaisons between the two are not unknown, for example Syria.

It is not unreasonable to think of Islam as 'spiritual communism'.

D

Dynamic Equivalents

These are devices to help our Muslim friend grasp Bible truth. For example the issue is not Muhamad versus Jesus. The dynamic equivalent of Muhamad in Christianity is Mary not Jesus.

- The Koran is the 'word made book' while Jesus is the 'word made flesh'.
- Muhamad gave birth to the 'word made book' and Mary gave birth to the 'word made flesh'.

F

Feast Days

The Arabic word for "feast" is *Eid*, which means "returning at regular intervals". These are usually public holidays in Muslim countries. It goes down well to greet

Muslims on feast days with the words in Arabic "*Eid al-mubarak!*" (Blessed feast to you!). You can find out the dates of the feasts from your Muslim contact. Here are the more important feasts.

- **Eid ul-Adha** (Feast of Sacrifice) Commemorates Abraham's near sacrifice of his son. Islamic tradition says it was 'Ishmael' while the Bible clearly says it was Isaac (Gen 22). On this occasion a sheep or goat (1 per household), cow or camel (1 per 7 households) is sacrificed in an halal fashion. One third of the meat is consumed by the household and the remainder is distributed to friends or the poor.

- **Lailat ul-Bara'at** (Night of full-moon before Ramadan - 14 Shabaan)

- **Ramadan** (Lunar month) Designated as the annual fast from sunrise to sunset

- **Lailat ul-Qadr** (Night of Power - 27 Ramadan) The last Friday night of the month of Ramadan when Muslims believe Gabriel began to reveal the Qur'an to Muhamad. Muslims are sometimes open to the supernatural assistance of God at this time. Millions of Christians are now praying for Muslims during Ramadan and supernatural intervention is being reported in the lives of ordinary Muslims.

- **Eid ul-Fitr** (Feast of Breaking the Fast) Literally in Arabic, 'Feast of Breakfast'. A three or four day feast commemorates the end of the fasting month of Ramadan. This is the closest atmosphere the Muslim world gets to Christmas. Children often have new clothes and presents can be exchanged.

- **Lailat ul-Miraj** (Miraculous Night Journey 27 Rajab) A one-night event where devout Muslims meditate and reflect on Muhammed's supernatural journey.

- **Mawlid an-Nabbi** (Muhammed's birthday - 12 Rabi al-awwal) Devout Muslims commemorate Muhammed's life and achievements.

- **Muharram** (Muslim New Year, first month in the Islamic calendar) A bank holiday in Muslim countries.

- **10 Muharram** or Ashura (Shi'ite memorial of the martyrdom of Hussein)

- **Hajj** (Lunar month designated to pilgrimage to Mecca) Most Hajj pilgrims will set out for Mecca in this month as it is thought to carry maximum *baraka* (blessing).

Useful Words and Expanations

G

The Gospel of Barnabas

Muslims struggle with the idea of four written Gospels and their tradition says the original Injil (Gospel) was lost. It is assumed that Christians concocted four Gospels to replace the original. Some Muslims argue for the authenticity of a document first found in the Papal Library around 1590. It is now called the Gospel of Barnabas. It seems to have been written by an Italian between 1400-1500AD - probably a convert to Islam. The document attempts to endorse the Koran's version of the life and work of Jesus. The writer is someone who had knowledge of the 'apocryphal' traditions of both Christianity and Islam but little clue about the geography nor the historical context of Jesus or Muhamad. Its details therefore contradict both New Testament and Koran. The writer claims to be Barnabas and that he associated with Jesus.

The real Barnabas was only associated with Paul. This so-called 'Muslim Gospel' is a jumble of inaccuracies and even quotes from the work of the writer Dante who did not live until 1245-1321 AD.

H

Hygiene

Nasal discharge is thought by many Muslim cultures to be as unclean as urine or faeces. When a Muslim has a cold it is not uncommon for them to sniff rather than wipe or blow the nose. This is seen as more appropriate in a toilet. It is more common to spit or blow the nose outside as this does not make a house unclean.

M

Meccan & Medinan Suras

The early Suras were written in Mecca during the phase when the Muslim community were in the minority and opposed by the people. These tend to be more reasoned and deal with similar 'spiritual' issues to those addressed by the minor prophets of the Old Testament.

All other suras were 'received' in Medina. They tend to be more volatile and even aggressive in tone during a phase when the Muslim community was in the majority and powerful.

Mosque

Masjid is the word in Arabic. It is the 'gathering' or 'meeting' place and centre of the worshipping Muslim community.

Inside a mosque:

• There is a place to perform *wudu* (ritual washing).

• The men and women worship in separate areas screened off from one another. The women usually pray behind the men and sometimes even have their own entrance.

• The focal-point is the *mihrab*. This is a highly decorated recess in a wall giving the precise direction of Mecca. The wall in which this recess is built is called the *qiblah*.

• Sermons are preached from a mimbar (pulpit).

The usage of the mosque:

• Officially there is no clergy or hierarchy within Islam. Prayers can be led by anyone who becomes the *imam* - this can be simply a reliable and experienced Muslim, though it tends to be the well read Muslims who become known as *Sheikh* (elder) or *mu'allam* (teacher). These are like rabbi figures.

• Mosques often run after-school Qur'anic classes to teach Muslims youngsters their faith. This is called a *madrsah* (school). Some Muslim boys can recite the Qur'an by heart by their fourteenth birthday.

• Some mosques also provide recreational facilities for Muslim young people.

N

Names

Naming is a complex business in Muslim cultures. Names can come from the area of family origin, or from their family clan or their grand father or father's name. For example Usama bin Muhamad bin Laden means Usama "son of" Muhamad (his father) "son of" Laden (his grand father i.e. family name).

Males can change their name if they are seriously ill in the belief that this will confuse the *jinn* spirits who may wish to take advantage and kill them.

Boys names are often taken from…

1. the prophets of the Koran e.g. Ibrahim, Musa or Muhamad

2. the 'companions' of Muhamad e.g. Ali, Usman or Abu Bakr

3. the names of God e.g. Rahman, Rashid

Girls are often named after…

1. the honourable women mentioned in the Koran e.g. Sara or Maryam

2. the women from Muhamad's family e.g. Fatima or Khadijah

3. the names of God e.g. Azizah or Mahbubah

4. beautiful things in their native languages e.g. Shukria or Shireen

Useful Words and Expanations

Women may change their names several times through their life. For instance when they complete adolescence, when they marry and by the name of the first born son (Oum Ahmad or Mother of Ahmad).

P

Proclamatory Dialogue

This is not a theologically liberal stance, which might tempt us to go in search of points of agreement and compromise at all cost. Like the liberal stance, this form of dialogue does involve listening and genuinely trying to understand and learn. However, it differs in that it also involves having something to say (proclaim) in response to what we hear and learn from our Muslim friend.

The evangelical position is sometimes seen as bigoted and closed to the 'truth' of others. The fact is that, like the old saying, Christians are only 'beggars sharing bread'. This is the balance of proclamatory dialogue i.e…

a. We are *beggars* relating in humility.

b. We are *sharing* in dialogue not dictating in mono-logue.

c. There is such a thing as the objective *bread* of life to share.

R

Redemptive Analogy

Simply put, these are analogies of redemption. That is to say they are devices, which use what a Muslim friend knows and build on it to convey the truth about Jesus. Here are two examples…

- The Black Stone
  This is a smooth corner of old meteorite rock on which the Ka'aba is built in Mecca. It is the centre of hajj pilgrimage and Muslim veneration. The stone is black and shiny, which has led to the tradition that it became shiny and smooth by the kisses and stroking of millions of pilgrims and that it is black because when pilgrims kiss it their sins are transferred to it. Psalm 2 says 'kiss the Son'. Jesus is the Black Stone of Christianity. When we embrace Him by faith our sin is dealt with.

- Abraham's sacrifice
  In Genesis 22 Abraham is willing to offer his only son. Muslim tradition says it is Ishmael but it really doesn't matter. The issue is the ram in the thicket. The story outlines 'substitutionary atonement'. Jesus is the Lamb of God and was slain to save us from being slain. He brings us into relationship with God.

S

Sharia

This is Islamic Law, which is a parallel to the Old Testament law. The Arabic word *sharia* means pathway leading to water holes in the desert. Such a beautiful concept seems far from the reality that wherever sharia law has been attempted in modern times, it has introduced economic ruin, political chaos or bloodshed, or all three. For example Iran, Sudan, Pakistan and Nigeria. Sharia Law legislates for all human behaviour. Sin, personal vice and crime are all treated as one issue under the divine rule. The four sources of authority in Sharia Law are…

1. Koran - the revealed scripture

2. Hadith - the Traditions about Muhamad's life

3. Ijma - judgement based on the consensus of qualified persons

4. Qiyas - judgement based on the use of analogies with other cases

The theory behind sharia law is that, as the revelation of God, it provides everything the Muslim can ever need to determine how he or she should live. Sharia is a guide and bench-mark for everyday life. There are four different schools of interpretation of Sharia Law. The four sharia schools are …

a. Hanifi

b. Hanbali

c. Shafi

d. Maliki

The schools can cause controversy within a Muslim community. For example the huge internal disagreement as to how to respond to Salman Rushdie's book 'The Satanic Verses'. The differing schools can also create legal wrangling. For instance if a Muslim is not satisfied with one ruling he can go to a lawyer of another school to get the ruling he likes.

Source of Islam

The $64,000 question is - "What is the origin of Islam?". This is not easy to answer, however it is possible to narrow the field a bit and say that it can only come from one of three sources.

1. divine revelation

2. human conception

3. satanic imitation

Life is never straightforward and it is highly likely that Islam is actually a mixture. This calls for mature discernment on the part of Christians trying to befriend a Muslim.

Useful Words and Expanations

Apart from the 'spiritual sources' of Islam, the reasons for its birth and rapid development are various. However, we must remember that all of them, whether good, bad or indifferent, somehow fall within the sovereign purpose of God and therefore must have a place in the divine economy as did the holocaust, Hiroshima and Apartheid. The following pointers may be helpful.

1. The failure of a weak church of the time that was lacking in understanding of the Scriptures, moral purity and mission vision.

2. Islam as an 'Arabised' form of Judaism appealed to the Semitic Arabs.

3. Islam spread quickly largely along natural Arab trading routes and through what Christians today call 'tentmaking'.

4. Islam spread by political, economic and military force

5. Islam has spread through significant population growth

W

The place of women in Islam

It is clear that Islam, like the Old Testament, reveals a male-oriented culture. For example it is interesting to note that the Virgin Mary (Maryam) is the only woman to be mentioned in the Qur'an by name. In Islamic law, women tend to be held in a tension between being dutifully 'protected' and negatively oppressed. The women of Muslim societies have been called the "wind-sock" of the Muslim World. How they are treated is a clear indicator of which way the wind is blowing in any given situation. For example the harsh regime in Afghanistan under the Taliban was hard on women. This cultural practise comes partly from the same culture as the Old Testament where the honour and wealth of a family could be assessed by the number, modesty and chastity of its women.

However, it is right to point out that there appears to have been more involvement of women in the life of the Old Testament community than is true in conservative Muslim societies (see Deut 29:9-13; Neh 8:1-3; 2 Kgs 4;23, 22:12-20; Judges 4:4-5:31). Jesus' treatment of women was clearly preferential and emerged out of his relationship with them (see Mt 22:30, 27:55-56; Mk 12:40-44; Lk 7:36-50; Jn 4:7-27, 12:3-8).

Photo courtesy of Frontiers International©

Modesty:

In conservative Islam, women should not look at men nor reveal any of their body to a male other than her close family (S24:31).

Women are to remain in the home and whenever they go out to cover modestly with the hijab (S33:33). The hijab was originally a head covering but has traditionally grown to become total covering (purdah) in some Muslim societies.

Spiritually:

According to the Hadith most of those who go to hell will be women. (Bukhari Vol.1, pgs 48 & 301). Women are deficient in intelligence, religion and gratitude (Bukhari Vol.1, No.301)

Legal rights:

The Koran says…'women shall have rights similar to the rights against them…but men have a degree over them' (S2:228). Another aspect of this legal inequality is the fact that a woman's inheritance rights are half that of a man…'To the male a portion equal to that of two females' (S4:11) '…and if there are not two men, then a man and two women such as you choose for witness' (S2:282) and again… 'In what you leave (i.e. in legacy) the wife's share is a fourth if you leave no children; but if you leave a child the wife gets an eighth, after payment of legacies and debts' (S4:12).

In Christianity the Apostle Peter writes that 'women are the weaker vessel' (1 Peter 3:7). Sadly the reflection in Islamic tradition, is that the woman's dependency on the senior males in the household is …because of the 'deficiency of a woman's mind (Hadith Vol 3:826). A husband may therefore punish an errant wife…'Women on whose part you fear disloyalty and ill-conduct, admonish them and refuse to share their beds, beat them.' (S4:34).

Sexual practises:

One Hadith reports Muhamad as saying 'When a man marries, he perfects half of religion'. The Koran says 'Marry women of your choice, two or three or four.' (S4:3). There are also some disturbing references to women and sexual behaviour. For example 'The Prophet (i.e. Muhamad) married A'isha when she was six years old and co-habited with her when she was nine'. Another Hadith (Vol 6:51) says 'The Jews used to say if one has sexual intercourse with his wife from the back she will deliver a squint-eyed child; so this verse was revealed. "Your wives are a tilth (i.e. ploughed field). So approach her when and how you will" (see S2:223).

Women are seen as the possession of their husbands for his enjoyment (S3:14). A Muslim man may marry up to four wives provided he can treat them all equally (S4:3), which the Koran claims is impossible (S4:129).

Appendix 3
Resources

General assistance:

Global Connections - (formerly Evangelical Missionary Alliance), Whitfield House, 186 Kennington Park Road, London SE11 4BT Tel: 020 7207 2156, email: info@globalconnections.co.uk
For general help including access to the full list of organisations with expertise and experience in this field.

Prayer for Muslims:

FFM - (Fellowship of Faith for Muslims), PO Box 5864, Basildon, Essex SS13 3FF
For a monthly bulletin of information for prayer and an annual prayer conference.

Biographies of converted Muslims:

Captive of the Christ - Steven Masood, Gospel Literature Service, Bombay, 1984
A powerful account of conversion in Pakistan

I Dared to Call Him Father - Bilquis Sheikh, Waco, TX.: Word, 1978
A high born Pakistani lady finds Christ

Jesus: more than a Prophet - RWF Wooton (ed.), Inter-Varsity Press, Leicester, 1982. - Fifteen Muslims find forgiveness, release and new life.

Literature for use with Muslims:

CPO - (Christian Publicity Organisation) Garcia Estate, Canterbury Road, Worthing BN13 1BW Tel: 01903 263 354 email: info@cpo.org.uk
For greetings cards featuring appropriate Bible texts in Muslim languages

Islamic Quarterly Magazine
Islamic Cultural Centre & Central Mosque 146, Park Road, London NW8 7RG
www.islamicculturalcentre.co.uk
For an authentic journal from an Muslim source

'**Kitab**' - P.O. Box 16 Failsworth, Manchester M35 9QL Tel: 0161 678 6838 email: kitab.uk@domini.org
For Christian literature about Islam and material for use with Muslims in vernacular languages.

Light of Life - P.O.Box 13, 9503 Villach, Austria. For Arabic Christian literature.

MECO - (Middle East Christian Outreach) For Arabic Christian literature & video catalogue www.arabmultimedia.com

SGM - (Scripture Gift Mission International), Radstock House, 3 Eccleston Street, London SW1W 9LZ Tel: 020-7730-2155 e-mail: lon@sgm.org
For Scripture booklets in many languages spoken by Muslims.

The Muslim Educational Trust
130, Stroud Green Road, London N4 3RZ email: info@muslim-ed-trust.org.uk
For authentic information from a Muslim source

Word of Life - P O Box 14, Oldham OL9 7SQ
For Bible Correspondence Course to help a Muslim learn about the Christian Faith. Can also be used to nurture a believer from a Muslim background.

Material on cassette:

Language Recordings - PO Box 197, High Wycombe HP14 3YY Tel: 01494 485414 email: irukoffice@aol.com
Gospel tapes in most Muslim languages.

Training & Seminars:

All Nations Christian College - Easneye, Ware Herts, SG12 8LX Tel: 01920 461 243 email: mailbox@allnations.ac.uk
For an annual ten days residential Islamics training course at an intermediate to advanced level during December.

Faith to Faith - Carrs Lane Church Centre, Carrs Lane, Birmingham B4 7SX Tel: 0121 633 8860, email: faithtofaith@talk21.com

Friendship First - email: freindship2101@aol.com
Steve Bell's consultancy - a resource and training service for the local church.

Centre for Islamic Studies & Muslim Christian Relations - London Bible College, Green Lane, Northwood HA6 2UW Tel: 01923 456 160, email: cis@londonbiblecollege.ac.uk
For a distance learning course on Islam & Christian Witness.

Booklets and literature about Islam:

CLC (Christian Literature Crusade) - 51 The Dean, Alresford, Hampshire SO24 9BJ

KITAB - For stocks of the Koran and many titles about Islam. (see opposite)

STL (Send the Light) - PO Box 300, Carlisle, Cumbria CA3 OQS

WEC - (Worldwide Evangelisation for Christ International) Research Office Bulstrode, Oxford Road, Gerrards Cross, Bucks SL9 8SZ, Tel: 01753-884631 e-mail: patrickj@globalnet.co.uk
For information about particular countries and people groups. A wide selection of colour OHP acetates is available.

Materials to help Muslim Background People:

JMBB Bible study & nurture material - www.openmysight/firmanullah.com

Christianity explained to Muslims - www.biblicalchristianity.freeserve.co.uk

Some Muslim Propagation Websites:

Al-Azhar University - www.alazhar.org

Council on Islamic-American Relations - www.cair.com

Islamic Gateway - www.ummah.org.uk

Malcolm X Black Muslims - www.colostate.edu/Orgs/MSA/docs/m_x.html

Muslim Directory - www.muslimdirectory.co.uk

Muslim Women's Page - www.albany.edu/~ha4934/sisters.html

World Assembly of Muslim Youth - www.wamy.co.uk

Appendix 4
Islamic Words and Expressions

A-H

A	
abd	A male slave
abrogation	A principle of Koranic interpretation (see Useful Explanations)
ahl-al-kitab	People of the Book i.e. Jews and Christians
Allah	The Arabic word for God
al-hamdu lilah	Arabic for "Praise be to God" i.e. 'Praise the Lord!'
al-asr	The afternoon prayer time
arkan-ud-din	the pillars of religion i.e. the Five Pillars of Islam
athaan	The call to prayer
ayah	Used for a verse of the Qur'an. The Arabic for 'sign'. Ayat in Urdu.
Ayatollah	A term of honour for a Shiah religious leader. Literally 'sign of Allah'

B	
baraka	Blessing
begum	Pakistani word in the Urdu language. A respected married woman.
bismillah	Arabic for "In the name of God". Used before a Muslim does anything
burqa	Pakistani Urdu term for ladies clothing that covers the whole body including hands and face.

C	
Caliph	Derived form the Arabic name *Khalifa* or ruler of a Muslim community.
chador	The Persian word for *burqa*, the ladies clothing covering the whole body

D	
dahwah	Literally "invitation" or "appeal" and used for Islamic mission
dar ul-harb	The house of war i.e. the non-Muslim world
dar ul-islam	The house of Islam
din	Arabic for religion (i.e. the outward practise)
du'a	Petitionary prayer
dhimmi	All non-Muslims living in a Muslim country. Subjugated and sometimes forced to pay a tax (see *jizya*)

E	
Eid	Feast
Eid-ul-fitr	The feast of "break-fast", which marks the end of Ramadan, the lunar fasting month
Eid-ul-adha	The name for the Sheep Feast. Also called Eid-ul-kibir. This is observed 70 days after the end of Ramadan
Eid-ul-milad	The name for the feast of the official birth of Muhamad and also of the birth of Jesus (Christmas)

F	
fajr	The early morning prayer time
falah	Self effort and positive achievement
fatiha	The opening chapter (sura) of the Koran
fatwa	A published opinion on a matter of Islamic law

H	
hadith al-qudsi	An individual "holy tradition" or trustworthy report on an action or opinion of Muhamad (see Hadith)
Hadith	The second holy book of Islam containing the *hadith al-qudsi*, a collection of traditions about the life and work of Muhamad. (see *isnad*)
hafiz	Someone who has memorised the Koran. Also a professional Koranic reciter
hajj	The annual pilgrimage to Mecca and Medina (see *hajji*)

hajji	Someone who has been on hajj. Men may dye their beards henna orange as a sign of this distinction (see *hajj*)
halal	Muslim equivalent of Jewish *kosher* food. Also used of food i.e. animal meat or fats obtained by slaughter invoking the name of God. Also something that is lawful and permissible.
haram	Something that is forbidden e.g. pork and alcohol. Also used for "shame on you" when someone does something inappropriate
harem	The female section of a Muslim household
higra	Muhamad's flight from Mecca to Medina happened in 622 AD. This became 1 AH "anno-higra" and marked this start of the Muslim calendar
hijab	An Arabic word for "partition" or "curtain". It is used of the head and face coverings worn my Muslim women
hilel	The crescent moon, symbol of Islam, which like Judaism, is based on the lunar calendar.
hizb	party or group e.g. "Hizb Allah", a radical Palestinian group

I

Iblis	One of the names used for Satan or evil. It is derived from *diabolos*
iftar	The breakfast" or evening meal enjoyed by fasting Muslims during Ramadan
ijma	A consensus or opinion of a recognised Islamic authority about the understanding or interpretation of the Koran
imam	The recognised leader of a mosque
iman	Faith
Injil	Literally "gospel" or "evangel". The book, which Muslims believe was revealed from God through Jesus
isha	The last of the five prayer times of the day. Performed after dark
isnad	A chain of people whose credentials lend weight to the reliability of a tradition (see Hadith).

J

janna	Arabic for "garden" and used for Paradise
jihad	To "struggle in the way of God" (S47:4,77), which can be expressed in doing good or violent acts (see *mujahid*)
jinn	A spirit entity either good, evil or neutral. They need placating and coercing to help the individual. Unofficial magical practitioners' help.
jizya	The tax payable by non-Muslims (*dhimmi*) in Muslim lands as a sign of their subservience to the majority culture
jumma	Friday - the holy day in which prayer is important

K

ka'aba	Literally "cube" in Arabic and used of the black draped edifice in the grand mosque in Mecca, a centre of pilgrimage
kafir	An unbeliever. The opposite of believer - (see *mu'min*)
kalima	Literally a "statement" used for the Islamic creed "There is no god but God and Muhamad is the apostle of God"
Khalifa	Islamic State ruled by Islamic Law
khutba	The sermon by the Imam after the Friday prayers
kismet	The lot in life assigned to the Muslim (fate)
Kitab	Used for both the Koran and the Bible. Literally 'book'
Koran	The holy book of Islam, also spelt "Qur'an". Literally 'Recitation'

L

Lailat al-Qadr	The Feast of the Night of Power observed on the last Friday night of the fasting month of Ramadan

M

Malam	A religious teacher used more in Africa
maghreb	The evening or sunset prayers. Used to name Morocco the most western edge of the Muslim World where the sun sets

Islamic Words and Expressions

Mahdi	A title meaning "the one who is rightly guided". He is almost a Messianic figure who is awaited, particularly by Shia Muslims
mansukh	A later revelation in either Koran or Hadith, which supersedes an earlier one (see *nasikh*)
matn	The actual text of a Hadith (see *isnad*)
Mecca	The birth-place of Muhamad and city of his early life. Now the epi-centre of world Islam and the place of pilgrimage (see *hajj*)
Medina	The city, 200 miles from Mecca, where Muhamad fled persecution to in the *Higra* (emigration). It is also a site for pilgrims.
mihrab	The point on a mosque wall, indicating the direction of Mecca, which is the direction for Muslim prayer (see *qibla*)
minaret	The slender tower attached to a mosque from where the muezzin calls the people to prayer. Today loud speakers are mostly used
miraj	The mystical night-time journey Muhamad is believed to have made to heaven. It is rather like the apostle Paul being transported to the seventh heaven
mizan	The scales on which everyone's good and bad deeds are weighed on Judgement Day (see *Yum al'akhirah*)
mosque	From the Arabic *masjid* or *gamaa* meaning place of gathering. It is the Muslim equivalent of a church building.
muezzin	The one who calls Muslims to prayer
Muharram	The first month in the Islamic calendar.
mujahid	In one sense all Muslims are *mujahid* as they uphold the five Pillars of Islam. But the term is used specifically to refer to someone who does active jihad i.e. a struggle in the way of God - sometimes military. The plural is *mujahideen*
mu'min	A 'true' believer i.e. practicing, whether Muslim or Christian (see *kafir*)
Muslim	A male follower of Islam. Literally "one who submits to God".
Muslima	A female follower of Islam. Literally "One who submits to God".
Mullah	A religious teacher used more in the Indo-Pakistan sub-continent

N

nabi	Arabic for a prophet. Used of Muhamad to persuade Jews of his day that he was in the authentic line of Old Testament prophets
nasikh	An earlier revelation in Loran or Hadith, which is replaced by a later on (see *mansukh*)

P

pbuh	Used in brackets after any mention of Muhamad in Muslim literature. It is short-hand for "Peace be upon him"
pir	A holy person who is saintly
purda	Literally "curtain". Used for the seclusion and the veiling of women

Q

qibla	The direction Muslims must face to pray i.e. towards Mecca
Qur'an	The holy book of Islam, also spelt "Koran"

R

raka'a	One round of Muslim prayer positions
Ramadan	The lunar month in the Islamic calendar in which the main fasting takes place
rasul	An apostle or messenger. One through whom a holy book is revealed. Used of Muhamad to persuade Christians of his day that he was in the authentic line of New Testament apostles

S-Z

	S
sadaqa	Voluntary offerings, usually on feast days, given in addition to the regular *zakat* (tithe)
salah	The ritual prayers of Islam performed five times daily
salam	The Arabic word for "peace" the counterpart to Hebrew "shalom". It is used as a greeting
saleeb	The Cross of Christ. Also used for the act of crucifixion
sawm	Fasting
shahada	The Islamic creed "There is no god but God and Muhamad is the apostle of God"
Shariah	Historically used to refer to a desert "path" leading to water. It now refers to Islamic religious law as the 'way' to live
Shaytan	Satan
Sheikh	An elder, leader, respectable or learned person in the Muslim community, a good word to attach to an older man's name to show respect. Used by Christian Arabs for a church 'elder'
Shiah	The Muslim group (Shi'ites) that believes the true successor to Muhamad was Ali, his closest male relative
shirk	The unforgivable sin in Islam of associating a person or an object with God
Sufi	The word comes from the Arabic "*suf*" (wool). It is used for a Muslim who is committed to experiential and mystical experience of God. The Sufis are also a sect within Islam. In some ways they are the 'charismatics' of Islam
Sunna	Literally "a trodden pathway". Used of the sayings and doings of Muhamad as found jointly in the Koran and the Hadith
Sunni	Literally someone who is "of the pathway". An orthodox follower of Islam
Surah	Literally a "series". Used for a chapter of the Koran

	T
Tahrif	The doctrine that the Bible was corrupted by Jews and Christians
Talmud	The Jewish traditional law. Could be seen as a parallel to Shariah law
tanzil	Literally "to descend". The process of revelation 'coming down' from heaven
tasbih	Muslim prayer beads with 33 beads - prayed through three times to give the 99 names of God
taqdir	Destiny, fate or predestination
taqiya	Disguising of your true beliefs when you are in a position of weakness
tawaf	A circumambulation of the Ka'aba in Mecca during hajj pilgrimage
Tawrat	The Old Testament in general but the Torah, i.e. first five books of the Bible, in particular

	U
Ulamma	The corporate theological community in Islam. The scholars
Umma	The worldwide community of Muslims

	W
wahy	Divine inspiration
wudu	Ablutions before prayer i.e. washing hands, feet and every orifice of the head

	Y
Yum al-akhirah	The Last Day i.e. the Day of Judgement

	Z
Zabur	Psalm(s)
zakat	Literally purification". Used for the obligatory charity or tithe to the local mosque
zuhr	The mid-day prayers i.e. the second of the day

Appendix 5
Background and Further Reading

Abd ul-Masih	Islam and Christianity, Daystar Press
N. Anderson	Islam in the Modern World - a Christian perspective, Apollos, 1990
Bickel & Jantz	Islam - a user-friendly approach, Harvest House Publishers, 2002
M. Burness	What do I say to my Muslim Friends, C.M.S.
Carey College	Islamic Study Course Series, Carey College, 1991
K. Cragg	The Call of the Minaret, Collins Flame Classics, 1986
C. Chapman	You go and do the same - Studies in relating to Muslims, CMS, BMMF & IFES, 1983
C. Chapman	Cross & Crescent - Responding the challenge of Islam, IVP 1995
C. Chapman	Whose Promised Land?, Lion Books, 2001
E. Challen	To Love a Muslim, Grace Publications
A. Cooper	Ishmael my Brother - a Christian introduction to Islam, Marc Monarch Publications, 1993
B. Dennett	Sharing the Good News with Muslims, ANZEA Publishers, 1992
R. Gidoomal	Sari 'n' Chips, MARC/South Asian Concern, 1993
M. Goldsmith	Islam & Christian Witness, Marc Europe, 1987
J. Goodwin	What Price Honour, Warner Books, 1994
J. Haines	Good News for Muslims - tools for proclaiming Jesus to your neighbour, Middle East Resources, 1998
D. Hesselgrave	Communicating Christ Cross-culturally, Zondervan, 1978
J. Hinds	Qur'an Word Studies - a DIY discussion kit, Word of Life
C. A. Mallouhi	Mini-skirts, Mothers and Muslims, Spear Publications, 1994
C. A. Mallouhi	Waging peace on Islam, Monarch books, 2000
C. Marsh	Love Will Find a Way, OM Books
C. Marsh	Share your Faith with a Muslim, Moody Press
N.I. Matar	Islam for Beginners, Adrift Book Company, 1992
T. Matheny	Reaching the Arabs - a felt need approach, William Carey Library, 1981
C. Moucarry	Faith to Faith - Christianity & Islam in dialogue, IVP, 2001
A Maurer	Christian-Muslim Dialogue & Evangelism, MERCSA 1997
B.A. Musk	Touching the Soul of Islam - sharing the gospel in Muslim cultures, Marc Monarch Publications,1995
B. A. Musk	The Unseen Face of Islam, MARC, 1989
B. A. Musk	Passionate Believing, Monarch Publications, 1992
L. Newbigin et al	Faith & Power, SPCK, 1998
R. G. Register	Dialogue & interfaith Witness with Muslims, WEC & Fellowship of Faith, 1979
C. Sell	The Historical Development of the Qur'an, People International
B. Sheikh	I Dared to Call Him Father, Kingsway, 1978
V. Stacey	Christ Supreme over Satan, Interserve
V. Stacey	Practical Lessons for Muslim Evangelism, Interserve
P. Sookhdeo (Ed)	Sharing Good News - the Gospel & your Asian Neighbour, Scripture Union, 1991
H. Spencer	Islam & the Gospel of God, SPCK, 1976
K.L. Woodward	Article: 'The Bible & The Qur'an' in Newsweek, February 2002
A. Yusuf Ali	The Holy Qur'an, Text, translation & Commentary, The Islamic Foundation, 1975
M.A. Qazi	A Concise Dictionary of Islamic Terms, Noor Publishing House, 1989

Appendix 6
Allah - God of the Bible?

'After I came to know Isa (Jesus), it was like I was close to God and could speak easily to him. God became my father, my friend, everything... I don't have to have any rules like I did in the past.'

(Ahmad - Thailand, 2002)

Many Christians ask whether 'Allah' is the God of the Bible or not. It is a critical question because how you answer it will determine everything else about your response to Muslims.

Your answer will depend on whether you take an 'apologetic' or a 'polemic' approach to Islam. By this we mean whether you look for the similarities or the contrasts between Islam and Christianity.

The 'apologist' tries to construct a bridge on which a Muslim friend can approach us and discuss our two approaches to God. The 'polemicist', on the other hand, is more interested in the differences between us and tends to compare Islams weaknesses with Christianity's strengths.

However, the 'apologist' is not just a wishful thinker because there are objective reasons why the word "Allah" could be used to refer to God and that it is actually referring to the God of the Bible. Let's look at some of the justification for this.

Linguistic evidence:

Linguistically, Allah is the common Arabic word for God. It was used long before Islam began, which is why one of Muhamad's relatives was called "Abdullah" (servant or slave of God). Allah is also used by millions of Arabic speaking Christians today as well as by Christians in Muslim influenced lands like Indonesia and Central Asia.

Semantic evidence:

Bible translators tell us that over 1,000 different words are used around the world for 'God'. Almost all of them were adopted from existing 'pagan' terms; for example the Greek 'theos', Latin 'deus' and even our English Teutonic word 'God'. The semantics (i.e. 'meaning') of all these was borrowed and refined over time until they were filled with the biblical meaning. Because Muslims use 'Allah' but don't appreciate its full biblical meaning, is no reason assume Allah is not God.

Historic evidence:

The word 'allah' comes from the Arabic el-illah (the God). The High God (i.e. El) was understood throughout the Middle Eastern lands for centuries before Abraham. This is why we find the Hebrew names of Yahweh in the Bible include it - El-elyohn, El-shaddai etc.

For this reason the name Allah did not need introducing when Muhamad recited the Koran; it was already known. Also the idolatrous Arabian society at that time deified the planets. Not surprisingly Allah, as High God, was identified with a major planets (e.g. the moon). Allah was also understood to be the lord of a dynasty of lesser gods, which is called 'honotheism'.

Allah was said to have three daughters, Al-Lat, Al-Uzza and Menat (S 37:149-153; 16:59; 17:41-42). These deities were worshipped along with Satan and 'jinn' spirits (S 4:116,117; 6:100). The fairytale Jinni of Aladdin's lamp is based on this spiritual reality. All this is part of 'animistic' culture in which, to this day, the spirit realm is deeply respected and manipulated by rituals to gain practical help in daily life.

Remember that God called Abraham when he was part of this sort of culture in Ur of the Chaldeans. This spiritual cocktail also explains Rachel's "household idols" (Gen 31:30-35) and the presence in Jacob's household of "foreign gods" alongside worship of Yahweh (Gen 35:2-4).

'Those who say that Allah is not the God and Father of our Lord Jesus Christ are right if they mean that he is not so described by Muslims. They are wrong if they mean that Allah is other than the God of the Christian faith.'

Bishop Kenneth Cragg

Logical evidence:

If Allah is the God of the Bible semantically, the next question is whether the spiritual reality behind the name 'Allah' is the same as that behind the name 'El'. It is clear that a particularly violent spiritual reality is present within the system of political Islam today. But this does not mean that Allah is the person behind this darkness, any more

The Origin of the name of God in the Middle East

El	= the ancient high god of the Middle East
Elah (Dan 2:45)	= Aramaic word for God (Yahweh)
El-yohn (Gen14:18-20)	= Hebrew word for 'Most High God' (Yahweh)
'alah (root of el-yohn)	= Hebrew word "to ascend" or "be high"
El-ilah or Allah	= Arabic word for 'High God'